D1609251

MAUI COOKS AGAIN

By Gini Baldwin, Judy Bisgard, Judy Furtado, Zelie Harders, Carol Hartley, and Penny James. Historical narratives by Kaui Philpotts. Graphic design by Jill Richards Weed.

Illustrations by George Allan, Pam Andelin Cameron, Cynthia Conrad, Betty Hay Freeland, Ben Kikuyama, Jan Kasprzycki, Al Lagunero, Diana Lehr, Richard Nelson, Macario Pascual, Ann Uyehara, and Scott Burns. Black and white illustrations by Joe Crabtree of Art Parts.

Maui Cooks Again is a continuation of *Maui Cooks*, presenting more of our treasured recipes. They come from old time celebrations and traditions, from multi-cultural experiences and friendships, and from the past ten years of trying to eat "lean and healthy."

Published by Maui Cooks Inc., 461 Aulii Drive, Pukalani, Maui 96768

Title Type: Neuland, circa 1923. Produced by Klingspor Type Foundry.
          Designed by Rudolf Koch.
Text Type: Garamond

First Printing 1994
Printed in Hong Kong

ISBN 0-9639120-0-3

DEDICATION

We dedicate this book to the Maui Community Arts and Cultural Center, as a celebration and a salute to the creative spirit, with hope and joy and gratitude for all that the Center will bring to Maui. May it flourish, nurturing the mind and soul, teaching, encouraging, inspiring, delighting and enriching; and may it bring together in one spot the diverse cultures that make up our community.

PAMELA ANDELIN CAMERON

Upcountry on a Kona Day. Pineapple Fields. Oil by Pamela Andelin Cameron.

Pineapple has a way of hugging the contours of the land, rolling and dipping effortlessly. A sea of colorful blocks making a tidy pattern on the face of the island.

The descendants of missionaries introduced pineapple cultivation to the islands in the later part of the last century. They set up plantations on what had been barren, or ranch lands, brought in water with ditch systems, established canneries, and shipped both the canned and fresh product to be enjoyed on the mainland. The pine they grew came to represent Hawaii. It was sweet and juicy and it tasted like sunshine.

The end of the summer harvest called for a celebration with the entire community participating in games, watermelon eating contests, and the preparation of food. In the old days, an *imu,* or cooking pit, was dug. *Laulau* and other island delicacies were cooked underground and enjoyed by all.

DYNAMITE!

Judy discovered this in San Diego a few years ago and it has become a favorite. It is particularly delicious, if a bit messy, served as a pupu with pieces of crusty bread that can be used to sop up the wonderful sauce. The name says it all, a firecracker beginning to any meal.

1 pound bay scallops,
   or large ocean scallops cut into quarters
1 small Maui onion, minced
1 small zucchini, cut into 1 inch match sticks

⅔ cup mayonnaise
1 tablespoon chili powder
1 teaspoon Tabasco
Parmesan cheese

Lightly toss scallops, onion and zucchini. Spoon into six small, oven-proof dishes. In small mixing bowl, combine mayonnaise, chili powder and Tabasco. Top each dish with mixture.
Sprinkle generously with Parmesan cheese and broil under broiler until brown and bubbly.
Serves 6

LILY LING'S WINGS

The combination of rosemary, five spice and cayenne give the wings a unique taste, and oven cooking is very easy. If you have a barbecue in mind, however, these do well on the grill.

4 cloves of garlic
1½ teaspoons salt
1 tablespoon Chinese five spice powder
2 teaspoons paprika

1 teaspoon crumbled dried rosemary
½ teaspoon cayenne, or to taste
2 tablespoons vegetable oil
4 pounds chicken wings or drumettes

Using garlic press, press garlic cloves into a large ziplock plastic bag. Add salt, five spice, paprika, rosemary, cayenne and oil and mix and mash into a paste. Add chicken wings and coat evenly with marinade. Close ziplock bag and refrigerate for 4 hours or overnight.

When ready to serve, preheat oven to 425 degrees. Arrange chicken, skin side up, on foil lined large broiler pan and bake in upper third of oven for 25 minutes, or until golden brown.

Chicken may be prepared one day in advance, kept covered, chilled and then reheated, but it is best served immediately.

LOMI LOMI CALAMARI

An easy do-ahead appetizer for a refreshing surprise and change from the traditional lomi salmon.

6 pounds cleaned calamari
1½ cups finely minced onion
3 cups finely chopped tomato, seeded
  and drained
½ cup finely chopped green onion

1 cup finely chopped parsley
¼ cup fresh lemon juice
1½ tablespoons Hawaiian rock salt
1½ tablespoons coarsely ground pepper
½ cup olive oil

Cut calamari tubes into ¼ inch rings and boil in salted water for about 5 minutes.
Drain, rinse, drain again, cool and combine with remaining ingredients. Refrigerate.
Serve on toasted French bread rounds.
Cleaned calamari tubes are available at your fish counter.
Serves 20

LOMI SALMON DIP

Too good to be true.

Purchase:
4 ounces of prepared lomi salmon
1 8-ounce package of cream cheese
1 bag of taro chips

Drain salmon. Set aside 1 tablespoon.
Put the rest in a blender along with the cream cheese and pulse until just mixed.
Put into a pretty bowl and decorate with the reserved lomi salmon.
Surround with taro chips and serve.

OYSTERS WAILEA

Prepare early in the day, refrigerate until the last minute. Pop under the broiler as your guests arrive and listen to the ooooohs and aaaahs as your friends clamor for more.

12 fresh oysters in the shell
    or 12 oysters bottled, if fresh not available
12 tablespoons red cocktail sauce
12 tablespoons real bacon bits
12 tablespoons grated Parmesan cheese

Shuck oysters and arrange on the half shell on a broiler pan. Top each oyster with 1 tablespoon each of cocktail sauce, bacon bits and Parmesan cheese. Broil 7 to 10 minutes or until brown and bubbly. Arrange on a platter of seaweed, if available. If bottled oysters are used, place oysters directly on broiler pan and remove to a crisp crouton when done.
Serves 6

MAUNA KEA SHRIMP

We first had these at our Christmas party several years ago. Beautiful, fresh tasting and easy to assemble, they quickly became a mainstay for everyone's entertaining.

1 pound (this is about 20) medium shrimp,
   cleaned and deveined
1 teaspoon salt
20 Chinese snow peas, blanched
1 small bunch mint
1 small bunch basil
1 small bunch Chinese parsley
20 toothpicks

Peanut dip:
2 tablespoons chunky peanut butter
3 tablespoons vinegar
¼ cup soy sauce
1 tablespoon sugar
2 teaspoons fresh lime juice
1 mashed Hawaiian chili pepper
   or Tabasco sauce to taste
1 clove garlic, finely minced

Cook shrimp in 1 quart boiling water with 1 teaspoon salt added until shrimp turn pink. Immediately plunge shrimp into ice water. Drain and pat dry. On each shrimp lay a mint leaf, a parsley sprig and a small basil leaf. Wrap each shrimp around the middle with a snow pea pod and skewer with a tooth pick. Cover and refrigerate until ready to serve.
Dip: Mix all ingredients together and serve the dip in a bowl with the skewered shrimp placed around the bowl on a platter.
Yields 20

POISSON CRU CHINOIS

Judy entered this great pupu in a cooking contest on the Big Island and won first prize!

2 ½ pounds Ahi, cut into ½ inch cubes
2 to 3 limes
¼ cup Hawaiian salt
Dice the following: 3 green onions,
1 medium carrot, 1 medium Maui onion,
2 large cucumbers, peeled and seeded,
2 large tomatoes, seeded

Dressing: 1½ tablespoons minced ginger
⅓ cup oil
2 tablespoons lime juice
6 teaspoons sugar
2 packages long rice noodles
¾ cup oil
Chinese parsley for garnish

Squeeze limes and mix with Hawaiian salt. Add fish, toss well and marinate, refrigerated, for one hour. Rinse fish, blot dry and toss with the diced vegetables. Cover and return to the refrigerator. Make dressing. Set aside. Fry noodles: In a 12 inch frying pan or a wok heat oil to 375 degrees or test the heat by dropping one noodle into the oil. It should puff and float instantly. Add the noodles to the hot oil in batches. It will take only seconds for them to puff and turn white. Remove immediately and drain on paper towels. This step can be done ahead and noodles put in an airtight ziplock bag. To serve: Arrange layer of long rice on platter. Shake vinaigrette, pour on fish and vegetables and toss. Arrange mixture on top of long rice, garnish with chopped Chinese parsley. Provide small plates with chop sticks or forks. Serve immediately. You don't want to let the noodles get soggy. Serves 20

ROASTED GARLIC PATÉ

In our never-ending search for new and interesting pupus, this is our current favorite. It should be served at room temperature, so make it shortly before you need to use it. Do not refrigerate.

2 large heads of garlic
½ pound Mozzarella cheese, at room
   temperature, cut into one inch cubes

1 teaspoon freshly ground pepper
2 to 3 tablespoons extra virgin olive oil

Preheat oven to 300 degrees.
Wrap the unpeeled garlic heads individually in a double thickness of aluminum foil and roast in the middle of the oven for about 45 minutes. Set aside until cool enough to handle. Remove foil and separate the cloves. They should be soft.
Turn on food processor and working over the bowl, pinch the garlic cloves one by one, letting the roasted garlic fall into the bowl and discarding the skins. Add the cheese a square at a time until mixture is quite thick. The amounts vary depending upon the size of the garlic heads. You may not need to use the full ½ pound. With the machine still running, add the pepper and the olive oil, a tablespoon at a time, until the mixture resembles softly whipped potatoes.
Serve with crackers or slices of fresh French bread.
Yields 2 cups

BOBOLI WITH PESTO AND PROVOLONE

This is a particularly good substantial pupu. Sometimes we serve this with cocktails, sometimes with soup or salad for a light meal, and sometimes as part of a buffet.

1 12-inch boboli
1 cup pesto
5 ounces Provolone cheese,
  thinly sliced or shredded

Preheat oven to 400 degrees.
Spread pesto evenly over entire top of Boboli. Top pesto with Provolone cheese.
Bake on cookie sheet for 15 minutes, or until cheese melts.
Put under broiler for a minute or two until lightly browned.
Slice in wedges to serve for lunch or cut into smaller pieces for a pupu.
Serves 8 to 10

THAI CHICKEN BOBOLI

The combination of Asian seasonings and Italian cheeses makes this a truly exotic pizza.

Marinade:
1 small bottle teriyaki sauce, about 6 ounces
1 teaspoon lime zest
1 teaspoon crushed red pepper
3 large sprigs cilantro
⅓ cup fresh lime juice
2 tablespoons chunky peanut butter
2 tablespoons peanut oil

3 boneless, skinless chicken thighs cut in slivers
1 12-inch boboli
¼ cup hot chili oil, divided
1½ cups shredded Italian Fontina cheese
1½ cups shredded Mozzarella cheese
4 green onions, thinly sliced
1 carrot cut into fine julienne
1½ cups mung bean sprouts
½ cup coarsely chopped dry roasted peanuts
⅓ cup chopped fresh cilantro

Marinate chicken overnight. In a medium saucepan cook chicken in marinade until tender, about 5 to 7 minutes. Drain. Preheat oven to 400 degrees. Brush boboli with 2 tablespoons hot chili oil, then top with a layer of the cheeses, leaving a ½ inch border around edges. Strew the chicken over the cheeses and sprinkle with the green onions, carrot, bean sprouts and peanuts. Drizzle with remaining hot chili oil and bake for 8 to 10 minutes until bubbly. Slice and garnish with chopped cilantro.
Serves 8

YAM BISCUITS WITH SMOKED TURKEY

For the biscuits:
2 cups all purpose flour
1 tablespoon baking powder
1 teaspoon salt
2 tablespoons sugar
½ cup vegetable shortening
2 17-ounce cans yams, drained and mashed
2 tablespoons heavy cream

For the chutney butter:
½ cup unsalted butter, softened
4 scallions, minced
¼ cup minced bottled mango chutney
1 tablespoon Dijon-style mustard, or to taste

1 pound thinly sliced smoked turkey breast

Preheat oven to 400 degrees.
In a food processor combine flour, baking powder, salt and sugar. Add shortening and yams and blend until a soft dough is formed. Pat the dough ½ inch thick on a floured surface and with a floured 2 inch cutter cut out as many rounds as possible. Form the scraps into a ball, pat out and cut again. Put all the rounds on buttered baking sheet, brush lightly with the cream, and bake for 18 to 20 minutes, or until they are lightly colored. Transfer to a rack to cool.
Make the chutney butter: In a small bowl cream together the butter, scallions, chutney and mustard.
To serve: Split the biscuits, spread each with chutney butter and sandwich folded sliced of turkey between the biscuit halves. These may be made 1 day ahead and kept covered and chilled. Heat the sandwiches, wrapped in foil, in a preheated 350 degree oven for 15 minutes or until heated through. Yields about 24 sandwiches.

SUN DRIED TOMATO PESTO

This is a spectacular dip for tortellini. It is also wonderful with cold poached scallops or with sliced fresh vegetables . . . particularly green bell peppers.

¼ pound pepperoni, diced
3 tablespoons Dijon mustard
4 cloves garlic
1 to 2 tablespoons fresh lemon juice

1 tablespoon fennel seeds
7 ounces sun dried tomatoes, packed in oil
½ cup olive oil

Place pepperoni, mustard, garlic, lemon juice, fennel seeds and tomatoes with their oil in a food processor fitted with a steel blade. Process until smooth. Using only as much oil as the mixture can absorb, with the machine running, pour a thin, steady stream through the feed tube and continue processing until the mixture is smooth. You may not need to use all the ½ cup of oil. Serve at room temperature with warm tortellini or cold vegetables.

SPINACH GRUYERE TORTA

1⅓ cups fine, dry bread crumbs
¼ cup plus 1 tablespoon butter, melted
1 10-ounce package chopped spinach, thawed
3 8-ounce packages cream cheese, softened
¼ cup whipping cream
½ teaspoon salt
¼ teaspoon ground nutmeg
⅛ teaspoon ground red pepper

4 eggs
4 ounces Gruyere cheese, shredded
3 tablespoons green onion, minced
1 cup finely chopped ham
3 tablespoons butter
½ pound fresh mushrooms, chopped
¼ teaspoon salt
¼ teaspoon pepper

Preheat oven to 350 degrees.
Combine melted butter and bread crumbs, mixing well. Press into bottom and up sides of a well greased 10 inch springform pan, or into a 9 x 13 x 2 inch pan. Bake for 8 minutes. Remove from oven and let cool. Reduce oven heat to 325 degrees.

SPINACH GRUYERE TORTA

Drain spinach well, pressing between paper towel until barely moist. Set aside.

Combine cream cheese, whipping cream, ½ teaspoon salt, nutmeg and red pepper in container of an electric blender or food processor. Cover and process until smooth. Add the eggs and once more process until smooth. Place half of this cream cheese mixture into a small bowl and combine with the Gruyere cheese. Set aside.

Place the other half of the cream cheese mixture in a bowl with the spinach, onions and ham. Stir well. Set aside.

Melt 3 tablespoons butter in a medium saucepan. Add mushrooms. Cook over low heat, stirring frequently, until mushrooms are tender. Add ¼ teaspoon of salt and pepper. Set aside.

To assemble: Pour spinach mixture into crust. Layer drained mushrooms over spinach.

Carefully pour the cream cheese and Gruyere mixture over mushrooms. If using a springform pan, place cake on a baking sheet and bake at 325 degrees for 1¼ hours. If using a flat rectangular pan, reduce cooking time to 45 minutes. Turn oven off, partially open oven door, and leave cheesecake in the oven for 1 hour. Let cool to room temperature on a wire rack.

Serves 12 to 16

SPANISH SOUP

This is really a fun soup to serve. A great way to end a cocktail party!

Soup:
1 tablespoon olive oil
1 large Maui onion, sliced
1 clove garlic, minced
1 tablespoon flour
1 16-ounce can tomato purée
7 cups beef broth
½ cup white wine
1 teaspoon garlic salt
1 teaspoon sugar
1 teaspoon fresh oregano
1 teaspoon fresh basil

Toppings:
3 hard boiled eggs, chopped
1 cucumber, diced
1 bell pepper, diced
2 tomatoes, diced
2 carrots, grated
1 can garbanzo beans, drained
1 can sliced olives
1 cup sour cream
3 Italian or Portuguese sausages,
    cooked, drained and chopped

Sauté onion in olive oil over low heat until transparent. Add garlic. Stir in flour, then tomato purée.
Slowly add the beef broth, then wine, garlic salt, sugar, oregano and basil.
Simmer for at least 40 minutes to let flavors blend.
Serve like a curry, letting each person select the topping for his own bowl of broth.
Serves 6 to 8

SMOKED CHICKEN SOUP

As children we had black bean soup, thick and dark puréed beans with slices of hard boiled egg and lemon on top. The next two soups use black beans, but they are as different as night and day from each other and from the old fashioned soup of our youth. This one is rich, smoky and elegant.

½ cup unsalted butter, divided
½ cup carrots, diced
½ cup onions, diced
½ cup celery, diced
1 cup broccoli stems, peeled and diced
2 teaspoons dried thyme
2 teaspoons dried oregano
1 teaspoon dried sweet basil
¼ cup dry white wine

4 cups chicken stock, hot
1 tablespoon Worcestershire sauce
½ teaspoon Tabasco
1 cup smoked chicken, diced
1 cup cooked black beans
1 cup broccoli florets
2 cups heavy cream
Salt and ground black pepper to taste

In ¼ cup butter sauté carrots, onion, celery and broccoli stems for 5 minutes. Add thyme, oregano and basil; sauté 5 minutes more. Add wine and deglaze pan. Add hot chicken stock and reduce by one third. Add Worcestershire sauce, Tabasco, smoked chicken, beans and broccoli florets; simmer 5 minutes. Add cream and simmer 5 minutes more. Season to taste. Drop in remaining butter, piece by piece, stirring until melted and serve immediately.
Serves 6 to 8

BLACK BEAN SOUP

This soup is hearty and comforting. The roasted red peppers give a special punch, but they are not critical, if you are not fond of peppers.

1 cup dried black beans
8 cups chicken stock, divided
2 small bay leaves
¼ cup olive oil
1 large onion, coarsely chopped
1 small garlic clove, finely chopped
1 cup drained and chopped canned tomatoes
2 tablespoons red wine

1 teaspoon sugar
¼ teaspoon black pepper
1½ cups elbow macaroni
2 large red bell peppers, roasted, peeled and cut into medium dice (a generous ½ cup bottled roasted red peppers can be substituted)
1 bunch finely chopped flat leaf parsley
1 bunch chopped green onion for garnish

Wash and pick over beans. Cover with an inch of water and bring to a rapid boil. Boil for 2 minutes and turn off heat. Allow to sit covered for 1 hour. Drain beans and cover with 3 cups of the chicken stock. Bring to a boil and turn heat down to a simmer. Add bay leaves and cook until the beans start to get tender about 1½ hours.

BLACK BEAN SOUP

Meanwhile, heat the olive oil and sauté the onion until wilted and starting to brown. Stir in the garlic and continue to cook for another minute or so. Scrape the onion-garlic mixture into the beans and add the tomatoes. Continue cooking, adding more stock if necessary until beans are cooked. This can take up to an hour. Add wine, sugar, pepper and the balance of the stock. Stir together.

To serve, boil macaroni in salted water for 6 minutes. Drain and add to the bean mixture along with the diced red pepper. Simmer just long enough to completely cook the macaroni. Allow to sit for about 5 minutes before serving. Correct the seasonings. This should be a thick soup. Sprinkle with chopped parsley and green onion.

Roast Peppers: Halve, core and seed peppers. Flatten each half with the palm of your hand. Line a baking sheet with foil. Lay peppers, skin side up, in a single layer on the baking sheet. Place under a preheated broiler, about 3 inches from heat source, until skins are charred black. Remove to a paper or plastic bag. Seal for 15 minutes to steam peppers. Slip off charred skin.
Serves 6

PEAS, BEANS AND BARLEY SOUP

No meat, and it is never missed. The vegetable flavors are perfect all by themselves.

1 onion, diced
2 tablespoons olive oil
1 bay leaf
1 teaspoon celery seed
1 cup green split peas
¼ cup barley
2 quarts water
2 teaspoons salt
Pepper to taste

½ cup lima beans
1 carrot, peeled and chopped
3 stalks celery, diced
1 potato, diced
½ cup chopped parsley
½ teaspoon basil
½ teaspoon thyme
¾ cup Parmesan cheese, freshly grated

Sauté onion, bay leaf and celery seed in oil until onion is soft. Stir in peas and barley. Add water and bring to a boil. Simmer, partially covered, for about 90 minutes. Add salt and pepper, lima beans, chopped vegetables and herbs. Simmer another 35 minutes, adding water as necessary. Serve with freshly grated Parmesan sprinkled generously on each bowl.
Serves 6

OATMEAL SOUP

This is one of the few soups we know that tastes best when freshly made. Don't be put off by the unusual ingredients or the name. It is wonderful.

1½ cups regular rolled oats
6 tablespoons butter
1 large onion, minced
¼ teaspoon minced garlic

2 large tomatoes, chopped
1 teaspoon salt
6 cups chicken, turkey or lamb broth

Put oats in a large frying pan over medium heat and toast, stirring constantly, until they are lightly browned. Set aside in a bowl. Melt butter in frying pan and sauté the onions until transparent and soft. Add the garlic, tomatoes, salt, browned oats and the broth. Boil gently for 6 minutes, stirring occasionally.
Serves 6

LEAN SOUP

Dieting? Here's a hearty, delicious and easy soup for that week after the holidays or just before the big reunion.

1 46-ounce can tomato or V-8 juice
4 cups water
6 tablespoons beef bouillon powder
1 chopped onion
1 10-ounce package frozen, chopped spinach
1 10-ounce can button mushrooms, undrained

2 cups of any or all of the following vegetables:
   sliced cabbage or won bok, diced green
   bell pepper, celery, potatoes, beans, fresh
   basil and parsley
Salt and pepper to taste

Simmer gently until all the vegetables are cooked and flavors blended.
Serves 6

CHICKEN LUAU SOUP

A sophisticated soup based on the traditional flavors of chicken luau.

2 tablespoons vegetable oil
1 medium onion, sliced
2 cloves garlic, minced
5 slices fresh ginger, each the size of a quarter
2 quarts chicken stock

12 taro leaves, deveined
16 ounces raw chicken, cut in strips
1 tablespoon Hawaiian salt
1 teaspoon black pepper

In a one gallon soup pot sauté onion, garlic and ginger in vegetable oil until lightly browned. Add chicken stock and bring to a boil. Chop taro leaves in bite size pieces and add to boiling stock. Simmer for 1 to 1½ hours, until taro leaves are really tender. Remove ginger slices, add chicken strips, salt and pepper and cook for another 10 minutes.
Serves 6 to 8

CAULIFLOWER, JALAPENO AND CHEESE SOUP

The jalapeno comes through as an interesting surprise.

1 tablespoon butter
1 leek, white part only, chopped
1 small onion, chopped
2 stalks celery with leaves, chopped
½ teaspoon minced garlic
1 jalapeno pepper, seeded and minced

1 head cauliflower, florets only
4 cups chicken broth
½ cup shredded Cheddar cheese
1 cup half and half or whole milk
Salt and pepper to taste

Sauté leek, onion, celery and garlic in butter until translucent. Add jalapeno, cauliflower and broth.
Bring to a boil, then reduce heat and simmer 20 minutes, until cauliflower is cooked.
Place in blender and purée. Put purée in top of a double boiler, add cheese and cream or milk and
simmer over hot water, stirring until cheese melts and soup is smooth. Add salt and pepper to taste.
Serves 4 to 6

BUTTERNUT BISQUE

When you need a light and elegant soup, particularly around Thanksgiving, this is it.

1 butternut squash, about 3 pounds
1 onion
1 tablespoon butter
5 cups strong chicken broth
Salt and white pepper to taste
Chopped parsley for garnish

Croutons:
¼ loaf French bread, cubed
1 teaspoon minced fresh basil
1 clove garlic, minced
¼ cup butter

Preheat oven to 375 degrees.
Bake the squash whole for 1 hour or until tender. Cool, remove seeds and scoop squash into the bowl of a food processor. Sauté onion in butter until transparent and add to the processor. Purée squash and onion until smooth. Put purée into a pot and add chicken broth, salt and white pepper. Heat.
To make croutons: put bread cubes in a bowl. Sauté basil and garlic in butter briefly. Toss butter mixture with the bread cubes and then spread them on a cookie sheet. Toast in a 275 degree oven for 30 minutes, or until crunchy.
To serve, sprinkle each cup of soup with parsley and some croutons.
Serves 6 to 8

BETTY HAY FREELAND

Kaanapali Coffee. Oil by Betty Hay Freeland.

The slopes of the west side mountains were once just the bushy light green of sugar cane and neat rows of pineapple. But times change, and the world economy demands other products. Some are betting on coffee. Not the ordinary variety-but the kind bought at good prices in the gourmet markets of cities and the more chic towns.

Coffee that was once wild, is now planted and cared for, with one eye always on the larger market. It takes three years to have anything worth selling, but the coffee has started to show up in specialty booths at events on the island. It has much promise.

Kaanapali has come to suggest a good time in extraordinary luxury. Maybe the coffee will mean the same.

ANGEL HAIR PASTA WITH SHRIMP AND AVOCADO

Not just another pasta salad. This will be a favorite.

8 ounces cooked and chilled angel hair pasta
3 green onions, finely sliced
1 medium tomato, seeded and diced
3 tablespoons salted sunflower seeds
16 medium boiled shrimp, peeled and chilled
16 slices avocado
Cilantro for garnish

Vinaigrette Dressing:
½ cup orange juice
½ cup olive oil
1 minced garlic clove
1 minced Hawaiian red chili pepper, seeded
½ tablespoon cracked black pepper
½ teaspoon salt

Place all dressing ingredients in a food processor or blender and mix well.
Toss pasta, green onion, tomato and sunflower seeds in a bowl with ½ of the vinaigrette.
Mound pasta in the center of a plate and surround with alternate pieces of shrimp and avocado.
Drizzle remaining vinaigrette around pasta. Garnish with cilantro.
Serves 4

BACON BROCCOLI SALAD

Perfect summer staple for those impromptu evening barbecues.

2 pounds broccoli florets, blanched
¼ cup sunflower seeds
½ cup raisins
½ cup cooked and crumbled bacon

½ cup chopped green onions
½ cup mayonnaise
1 tablespoon vinegar
1 tablespoon sugar

In a large salad bowl combine broccoli, sunflower seeds, raisins, bacon and green onion.
Mix the mayonnaise, vinegar and sugar together. Add the dressing and toss just before serving.
Serves 6

CRAB BROCCOLI SALAD

2 pounds broccoli florets, blanched
½ pound crab or imitation crab
½ cup chopped green onion
½ cup mayonnaise
1 tablespoon lemon juice
1 tablespoon sugar

In a large salad bowl combine broccoli, crab and green onion.
Mix together the mayonnaise, lemon juice and sugar. Add to the salad mix and toss well.
Serve immediately or refrigerate for later use.
Serves 6

RED CABBAGE SALAD

A great cabbage salad. And there's no mayonnaise!

½ head red cabbage, about 2 pounds
½ cup parsley, finely chopped
2 tablespoons sherry wine vinegar
  or balsamic vinegar

¼ cup or more, olive oil
1 cup toasted walnuts, coarsely chopped
2 ounces Roquefort or Bleu cheese
Salt and freshly ground pepper to taste

Cut cabbage in half. Remove core and discard. Chop cabbage into shreds and place in bowl with parsley. Heat vinegar in a small pot and when very hot pour over the cabbage. Quickly toss, coating each piece thoroughly. Add the olive oil and salt and pepper. Toss again. Add walnuts and crumbled cheese. Toss once more and serve.
Serves 6 to 8

LEMON GINGER CHICKEN SALAD

A perfect luncheon for light appetites. Serve with our Boboli with Pesto and Provolone or Spinach Gruyere Torta for a more substantial meal.

Dressing:
1 tablespoon minced lemon zest
¼ cup fresh lemon juice
2 tablespoons ginger syrup*
1 tablespoon shoyu
½ teaspoon Chinese chili sauce or paste
2 tablespoons grated fresh ginger, lightly packed
1 clove garlic, minced
2 tablespoons vegetable oil
½ teaspoon salt

Salad:
10 won ton skins cut into ¼" strips
1 cup vegetable oil
1 pound boneless, skinless chicken breasts
10 large romaine leaves
1 cup shredded carrots
¼ cup chopped green onion

*Ginger syrup can be taken directly from a bottle of preserved ginger, or made by cooking together 2 tablespoons sugar, 2 tablespoons water and 1 teaspoon grated ginger.

LEMON GINGER CHICKEN SALAD

In a small jar, combine ingredients for the dressing. Cover tightly, shake vigorously and refrigerate.
In a large skillet or wok heat oil over moderate heat until it just begins to smoke.
Cook the won ton strips in several batches until light golden brown, about one minute.
Drain on paper towels.
Gently poach chicken until tender. Cool and slice chicken into thin pieces. Set aside.
Stack the romaine leaves and roll up from the long side into a tight cylinder.
Slice the roll at ⅛ inch intervals. Transfer the lettuce to a large salad bowl.
Add the carrots, green onions and the chicken. Shake the dressing, pour it over the salad and toss.
At the last minute, gently fold in the won ton strips. Serve immediately.
Serves 4

BARTLETT PEAR, FETA AND WALNUT SALAD

The pear salad is slightly sweet . . . .

Dressing:
2 tablespoons sugar
½ teaspoon grated onion
½ teaspoon dry mustard
½ teaspoon salt
¼ cup rice vinegar
½ teaspoon poppy seeds
½ cup canola oil

2 heads butter lettuce, torn into bite sized pieces
3 ounces crumbled feta cheese
½ cup chopped walnuts
2 large Bartlett pears, peeled, cored and sliced

Prepare dressing and set aside.
When you are ready to serve, toss the salad ingredients together, add dressing to taste and toss again.
Serve immediately.
Serves 6

AVOCADO PEAR, APPLE AND WALNUT SALAD

.....the apple salad is not.

Dressing:
⅓ cup red wine vinegar
⅔ cup olive oil
1 teaspoon Dijon mustard
1 teaspoon sugar
1 heaping teaspoon tarragon
2 cloves garlic, minced
½ teaspoon salt
½ teaspoon pepper

Salad:
1 bunch watercress and/or spinach,
 torn into pieces
1 head butter lettuce, torn into pieces
1 avocado, peeled and sliced
2 green apples, peeled and sliced
¼ cup coarsely chopped walnuts.

Place all the ingredients for the dressing in a jar and shake well.
Keep refrigerated. In a large salad bowl, place the watercress, spinach, lettuce, avocado and apple.
Shake the dressing and pour over the greens sparingly.
Toss lightly, sprinkle with walnuts and serve immediately.
Serves 6

KULA CARAMELIZED ONIONS

Take this on your picnic along with Bread Bowl Chicken and Tomato Feta Salad.

3 tablespoons olive oil
3 Kula onions, thinly sliced
1 tablespoon dark brown sugar
2 tablespoons red wine vinegar
Salt and freshly ground pepper
1 medium hard roll or small loaf of bread

Heat the olive oil in a cast-iron skillet.
Add the onions and cook over low heat, stirring occasionally, until they begin to brown, about 30 minutes. Add brown sugar, red wine vinegar, salt and pepper and cook 5 more minutes.
Slice off top of roll or loaf, remove spongy center, and spoon onions into bread.
Replace the top and wrap in a tea towel.
Serves 4

TOMATO FETA SALAD

To go with Bread Bowl Chicken and Kula Caramelized Onions.

1 pint basket ripe cherry tomatoes, halved
1 small red or Kula onion, thinly sliced
2 large cloves minced garlic
2 tablespoons olive oil

2 ounces feta cheese, crumbled
1 teaspoon freshly ground pepper
6 basil leaves, chopped
1 loaf dark crusty French bread

Toss the halved tomatoes with the sliced onion, garlic and olive oil.
Mix in the feta cheese, pepper and chopped basil. Slice off top of loaf and remove spongy center.
Spoon salad into bread. Replace top and wrap in a tea towel.
Serves 4

WON BOK SALAD

The mixture of mayonnaise and shoyu gives this salad a typical Island flavor.

1 head won bok, Chinese cabbage
  2½ to 3 pounds, shredded
½ pound fresh mushrooms, sliced
1 8-ounce can water chestnuts, sliced
4 to 5 green onions, chopped

1 5-ounce can crisp chow mein noodles
½ cup slivered almonds
¾ cup mayonnaise
4 to 5 tablespoons shoyu

Toast noodles and almonds for five minutes in a 350 degree oven or until crisp.
Mix mayonnaise and shoyu to make the dressing.
Toss the won bok, mushrooms, water chestnuts and green onions with the dressing.
Add the noodles and almonds just before serving.
Serves 6

CITRUS VINAIGRETTE

So many dressings for fruit salads are sweet. We were delighted to find this one.

½ cup fresh orange juice
¼ cup seasoned rice vinegar
1½ tablespoons fresh lime juice
1½ tablespoons fresh lemon juice

1 shallot, peeled and chopped
½ teaspoon freshly ground black pepper
¼ teaspoon salt
1 cup olive oil

In a food processor, combine the orange juice, rice vinegar, lime and lemon juices, the shallot, pepper and salt. Blend well. Add the olive oil slowly, processing until an emulsion is formed. Serve over greens and fruits of your choice.
Yields 2 cups

TED'S SPECIAL SALAD DRESSING

This is the only recipe Zelie's husband ever makes. It is a sweet and tart salad dressing that has been popular on Maui for years…as has Ted.

⅔ cup salad oil
⅓ cup sugar
⅓ cup catsup
⅓ cup wine vinegar

⅓ cup green onion, chopped
2 teaspoons Worcestershire sauce
Salt and pepper to taste

Yields: 1½ cups

LYCHEE SALSA

A knockout salsa! Particularly delicious served with grilled fish.

1 cup lychee fruit, fresh or canned
½ cup fresh papaya
⅓ cup fresh pineapple
⅓ cup red bell pepper
⅓ cup tomato, seeded and diced
½ cup water chestnuts, diced

3 green onions, chopped
¼ cup chopped cilantro
1 teaspoon Hawaiian salt
Juice of 2 limes
1 Hawaiian chili pepper, seeded and chopped

Dice all the fruit about the same size and mix with bell pepper, tomato, water chestnuts, green onion, cilantro, salt and lime juice. Add Hawaiian chili pepper to taste, and mix well.
Will keep for about a week in the refrigerator.
Serves 8

ANN UYEHARA

Kahului Shopping Center. Watercolor by Ann Uyehara.

It held such promise at a time when the plantation camps emptied their "chop suey" populations into one happy melting pot called "Dream City." The A&B Supermarket anchored one end and Ah Fook's the other. At lunchtime office workers showed up at Craft's or Toda Drug and took their places in the same old seats - year after year.

In the back corner of the Kahului Shopping Center, very early on weekends, fishermen pulled up to pick up bait, bento lunches, and last minute purchases before heading for the shoreline.

In the center courtyard was Harold's Inn, which seemed to just grow from its space in the building and spill out onto the asphalt. It claimed more space with booths made of cheap wood and painted an unusual shade of green.

These days, the sign along the road which once announced the special events is almost always missing critical letters. But the old men still gather to talk story and play cards under the monkeypod trees. Their picnic tables were removed years ago, but they come anyway. These men are old friends, and they like to keep in touch.

COCONUT SHRIMP

This is a simple creation that will have your guests raving. It looks especially beautiful served on a black platter.

1½ pounds large shrimp, peeled
1 green bell pepper, thinly sliced
1 red pepper, thinly sliced
1 yellow bell pepper, thinly sliced
2 tomatoes, peeled, seeded and chopped

1 clove garlic, minced
3 tablespoons butter
1 12-ounce can coconut milk
1 teaspoon tarragon
Salt and pepper to taste

Melt butter in a large skillet. Sauté garlic and peppers until just tender. Add shrimp, tomatoes, coconut milk, tarragon and salt and pepper. Simmer 2 to 3 minutes, turn heat off, cover with lid and let rest for 5 minutes. Serve with your favorite rice.
Serves 6

MOROCCAN FISH

Flavors of Morocco, plus a chef from New Hampshire, plus a cooking class on Maui equal a deliciously different treatment of Hawaiian fish: Mahi, Ono, or snapper.

2 teaspoons ground cumin
1 scant teaspoon ground coriander
1 scant teaspoon tumeric
¼ teaspoon cinnamon
1 teaspoon salt
Black pepper to taste
1½ pounds boneless, skinless fish filets:
   Mahi, Ono or Snapper

3 tablespoons olive oil
1 medium onion, chopped
2 cloves garlic, minced
1 cup chopped tomatoes, peeled and seeded
Juice of ½ lemon, or to taste
3 tablespoons chopped fresh cilantro,
   or flat leaf parsley

In a small bowl mix cumin, coriander, tumeric, cinnamon, salt and pepper. Rub ½ to ⅔ of the spice mixture into both sides of fish filets. Sauté onion and garlic in oil until soft. Add tomatoes, lemon juice and cilantro and simmer for 15 minutes. Add the balance of the spice mixture.
Spoon half of the tomato sauce into an oiled baking dish large enough to hold fish in a single layer.
Place fish on top, spoon remaining sauce over fish and cover with oiled foil.
Bake in a preheated 400 degree oven for 15 minutes, watch carefully so it does not over cook.
Serves 4 to 6

AHI PASTA

This is a favorite at any time of the year. However, when Ahi is expensive around holiday time this is a great way to make a little go a long way.

6 ounces Ahi, cut in small cubes
¼ cup chopped Maui onion
1 tablespoon blanched, chopped garlic
1 anchovy filet, chopped
2 teaspoons capers
½ cup chopped plum tomatoes

¼ cup chopped fresh basil
2 tablespoons chopped fresh oregano
3 tablespoons olive oil
Dash of pepper
8 ounces linguini, cooked

Briefly cook onion and garlic in the olive oil. Add remaining ingredients and sauté, stirring constantly, until the Ahi is barely cooked. Pour over hot pasta and serve immediately.
Serves 2

CRISP PANKO FILETS

The Japanese have a wonderful breading substance called panko. You might not be inclined to try it without a specific recipe. It is available in the oriental food section of most markets.

6 fish filets
1 cup flour
1 cup milk
1 small egg, well beaten
1 cup panko
4 tablespoons clarified butter

2 tablespoons lemon juice
2 tablespoons capers
½ teaspoon salt
1 clove garlic, minced
4 tablespoons butter

Lightly flour fish on both sides. Combine egg and milk. Dip fish in egg mixture. Roll in panko and sauté in clarified butter until the coating is lightly brown and crisp and fish flakes easily.
Make a sauce by warming lemon juice, capers and salt. Then add the butter which has been whipped with the minced garlic. Allow butter just to melt. Serve immediately.
Serves 6

SALMON CONFETTI

This is a great party entrée. It can be prepared ahead of time and then just popped in the oven as the guests arrive, cooking while you are enjoying cocktails.

1 3-4 pound salmon, butterflied
½ cup diced bacon, about ½ pound
1½ cups mayonnaise
1 Maui onion, diced
2 tomatoes, diced

½ pound mushrooms, sliced
A sprinkle of diced red and green bell peppers
2 tablespoons capers
Salt and pepper to taste
Juice of ½ lemon

Preheat oven to 425 degrees.
Put diced bacon in skillet and brown for 3 to 4 minutes over medium heat. Spread mayonnaise evenly on filet. Layer everything on top, in order given, ending with squeezed lemon over all. Cover tightly with foil and bake at 425 degrees for 35 to 40 minutes, or until fish flakes.
Serves 4 to 6

SALMON IN GINGER BUTTER SAUCE

This can be prepared several hours ahead of time and broiled at the last minute. A simple company dinner served with a green salad and sourdough rolls.

2 salmon filets, ½ pound each
3 tablespoons dry sherry
2 tablespoons light soy sauce
1 tablespoon oriental sesame oil
1 tablespoon finely minced ginger

2 tablespoons chopped fresh parsley
2 tablespoons butter
Salt and freshly ground pepper to taste
1 lemon

Combine sherry, soy sauce and oil. Rub filets with this marinade. Sprinkle ginger and then parsley across top of filets. Dot butter evenly across surface. Refrigerate until ready to serve.
To cook: Preheat oven to "broil." Salt and pepper filets. Put salmon on broiling pan and place about 4 inches below heat. Cook the salmon without turning until it turns a light pink and flakes with a fork, about 5 minutes. Garnish with lemon wedges.
Serves 4

MAUNALEI FISH

We think that this is an "original." We have never seen this combination of flavors used with fish anywhere else.

1½ pounds white fish filets:
   Mahi or Ono
½ cup flour
2 tablespoons butter
Salt and pepper

1 10½-ounce can beef consommé
2 tablespoons Dijon mustard
1 tablespoon lemon juice
2 tablespoons capers
2 teaspoons cornstarch

Dredge fish in flour, salt and pepper. Heat butter in frying pan and lightly brown the fish.
Combine consommé, mustard, lemon juice, capers and cornstarch.
Add to the fish and simmer until fish is just done. Do not over cook.
Serves 4

HAWAIIAN FISH STEW

Cioppino. Maui Style!

2 tablespoons olive oil
1 medium carrot, thinly sliced
1 onion, coarsely chopped
1 green bell pepper, seeded and coarsely chopped
2 stalks celery, sliced
1 clove garlic, minced
1 8-ounce can tomato sauce

1 28-ounce can plum or whole peeled tomatoes
1 cup dry red or white wine
1 bay leaf
¼ cup chopped fresh basil leaves
Salt and freshly ground black pepper to taste
1½ to 2 pounds of firm fleshed white fish:
    Ahi, Swordfish, Uhu, Uku

Heat the oil in a large pot. Sauté the carrot, onion, green pepper, celery and garlic until the onion is tender. Stir in the tomatoes with their liquid, tomato sauce, wine, bay leaf and basil. Season with salt and black pepper. Break up tomatoes with a spoon. Cook uncovered until slightly thickened, about 30 minutes. Discard bay leaf. Add fish, cover and simmer 8 to 10 minutes or until fish begins to flake. Serve with sourdough bread or over rice. Note: This recipe can be made up to 24 hours ahead. It can also be frozen.
Serves 6 to 8

PUFFY OMELET WITH CRABMEAT

This recipe came from the olden days when ladies entertained at luncheon parties. It makes a delicious light meal for any hour of the day or night, and chances are, you will always have the ingredients on hand.

6 tablespoons butter, divided in half
3 tablespoons flour
¼ teaspoon salt
Dash of pepper

1½ cups milk
1 6-ounce can crabmeat
2 tablespoons chopped parsley, divided
3 large eggs, separated

Melt butter in a medium skillet. Add flour, salt and pepper. Cook over low heat, stirring until smooth. Slowly add milk, stirring with a whisk to avoid lumps and cook until mixture thickens and comes to a boil. Remove from heat and stir in crabmeat. Take 1 cup of the crab mixture, reserving the rest for the sauce, add 1 tablespoon chopped parsley and 3 well beaten egg yolks. Beat egg whites until stiff but not dry, and fold into crabmeat mixture.
Melt the remaining butter in a large skillet. Pour the egg mixture into the skillet, cover and cook over medium-low heat until the omelet is puffed and looks cooked through. Slide out of pan onto a platter. Put half of the reserved crab sauce onto half of the omelet, fold in half and top with the remaining sauce. Sprinkle with the rest of the parsley and serve.
Serves 4

SHRIMP WITH PEANUTS

Once the shrimp are cleaned, this goes together in a flash and can be used as a pupu, or served with rice as a main course.

1 large garlic clove, minced
1 teaspoon peeled and grated ginger root
3 tablespoons butter
1 pound shrimp, shelled and deveined
6 scallions, thinly sliced

2 fresh red Hawaiian chili peppers, seeded and
   minced (don't forget to wear gloves)
⅓ cup roasted peanuts, chopped fine
1 teaspoon fresh lemon juice, or to taste

In a large heavy skillet cook the garlic and the ginger root in the butter over moderate heat, stirring, for 30 seconds. Add the shrimp and cook them, stirring for 30 seconds more, or until they are coated well with the butter. Reduce the heat to low and cook, covered, for 2 minutes. Stir in the scallions, the chili peppers, and salt to taste and cook for 1 more minute, or until the shrimp are just firm and pink. Stir in the peanuts and the lemon juice.
Serves 2 to 4

GEORGE ALLAN

Olowalu Paʻina. Oil by George Allan.

There are days that remind you of why you love the island. Days when the sun is bright above Olowalu, and the waves lap up on the shore with a quiet regularity.

The green lawn belongs to a family who've allowed it to be used as a fund raiser for a *halau,* or dance school. The oldtimers begin arriving with their lauhala hats to ward off the sun's rays, and fragrant leis they made at home from backyard flowers early that morning.

The friends and relatives of halau members begin bringing platters of seafood, salads, lomi salmon, poi and BBQ sticks to the canoes filled with ice and placed decoratively at intervals around the yard. They did the food themselves with the help of a relative who works as a chef at a nearby Kaanapali hotel. This is the real old Lahaina - existing quite nicely in and around the commercial one on display everyday for visitors. It will always be there because it's the residents that really make a community work. On the West Side they're still doing it.

CHICKEN CALCUTTA

This is one of those recipes that does best in small quantities. It is an elegant entrée for two or four people that takes only minutes to prepare.

2 large boneless, skinless chicken breast halves
2 tablespoons flour
¼ cup butter
½ teaspoon curry powder, or to taste
½ cup sliced mushrooms

¼ cup sliced green onions
½ cup whipping cream
3 ounces shredded coconut, toasted
Salt and pepper to taste

Slice chicken breasts into strips. Dust with flour until all are well coated. Melt butter in a large skillet and sauté chicken quickly over high heat until golden. Add curry powder to taste, then the mushrooms and green onions.
Cook, stirring and tossing, until the mushrooms are tender (1 to 2 minutes). Add cream, bring to a boil and immediately reduce heat and simmer until slightly thickened.
Season to taste with salt and pepper and serve sprinkled with the toasted coconut.
You should not add the cream until you are ready to serve the dish as the sauce will disappear if you don't move quickly at this point.
Serves 2

CHICKEN 'SPARE RIBS'

Our after-school sports teams have many potlucks after games. All ethnic groups are represented and this is a dish that has been popular with everyone.

2 pounds skinless chicken thighs or drumettes
1 teaspoon vegetable oil
½ cup water
⅓ cup shoyu
⅓ cup firmly packed brown sugar
¼ cup apple juice
2 tablespoons catsup or tomato sauce
1 tablespoon cider or rice wine vinegar

1 garlic clove, pressed
1 green onion, thinly sliced including top
½ teaspoon crushed red pepper
½ teaspoon freshly grated ginger
1 tablespoon cornstarch
1 tablespoon water
Green onion, sliced diagonally
Sesame seeds, toasted

Add oil to a large frying pan with nonstick finish. Heat pan over medium high heat until a few drops of water sprinkled on surface sizzle. Add chicken pieces and sauté, turning frequently, until lightly browned on all sides (about 5 to 7 minutes).
Combine next ten ingredients and add to chicken. Bring to a boil, cover and reduce heat. Simmer for 20 minutes. Blend together cornstarch and water. Add to chicken and cook, stirring, until sauce thickens and glazes chicken pieces. Garnish with green onion slices and sesame seeds, as desired.
Serve as a finger-food snack, or with hot rice as a main dish.
Serves 4 or 18 appetizers

CHINESE ROAST CHICKEN

Long a favorite of Pukalani Superette customers, it pops into a picnic basket for a day at the Crater, or it makes a fine dinner to pick up on your way home. It's even better right out of your own oven.

1 4-pound chicken
1 tablespoon oyster sauce
1 teaspoon salt
¼ teaspoon Chinese five spice

1 clove garlic, crushed
1 tablespoon shoyu
1 teaspoon brown sugar
1 slice crushed ginger, the size of a quarter

Rinse chicken and pat dry. Prepare the remaining ingredients and rub over the chicken, inside the cavity and out. Set aside in the refrigerator until you are ready to cook. For a more intense flavor marinate overnight.

About 1½ hours before you are ready to serve, remove chicken from the refrigerator and preheat oven to 350 degrees. Set chicken on a rack and pour any accumulated juices into the cavity. Roast until the skin is brown and crisp and the juices run clear when the chicken is pierced.

Serves 4 to 6

BREAD BOWL CHICKEN

For your next picnic, you can't beat this. You eat the chicken and the bowl and wipe your hands on the tea towel.

2 tablespoons butter
8 chicken thighs
Freshly ground pepper
¼ cup port wine
¼ cup orange juice

⅛ cup soy sauce
¼ cup cream
Zest of 1 orange
¼ cup chopped Italian parsley
1 large round loaf of French bread

Preheat oven to 350 degrees.
Melt butter in a cast-iron skillet and brown the chicken pieces. Sprinkle with pepper.
Pour the port, orange juice and soy sauce over the chicken. Transfer pan to oven and bake until done about 35 to 45 minutes. Remove chicken and set aside.
Return pan to stove. Pour cream into pan drippings and add half of orange zest. Reduce slightly over medium heat. Return chicken to pan and stir each piece in the mixture until coated. Slice off top of loaf and remove spongy center. Place chicken in the cavity. Sprinkle parsley and remaining zest over chicken. Replace top of bread and wrap in tea towel.
Serves 4

GUMBO

The beauty of this dish is the fresh taste and the ease of preparation. The chicken, shrimp, sausage, and green pepper can be prepared in advance and refrigerated in individual packets. A half an hour before serving, gumbo can be assembled quickly and neatly, and it is foolproof, even if done amid a swirl of guests who have followed you to the kitchen.

For Rice:
2 cups chicken broth
½ cup chopped onion
½ cup sliced celery
1 large clove garlic, crushed
1 cup long grain white rice

For Roux:
4 tablespoons butter
4 tablespoons flour

For Gumbo:
1 28-ounce can peeled, chopped tomatoes
3 chicken breast halves, boned, skinned and cut
    into 1½ inch pieces
½ pound Creole or Polish smoked sausage,
    in ½ inch slices
1 clove garlic, minced
2 bay leaves
1 teaspoon thyme leaves
¼ teaspoon cayenne pepper, or to taste
1 pound large shrimp, peeled and deveined
1 large green pepper, cut in ¾ inch squares
2 teaspoons filé powder

GUMBO

For Rice: Bring chicken broth to a boil. Stir in onion, celery, crushed garlic and rice. Reduce heat, cover tightly and cook until tender, about 25 minutes. Stir in parsley and keep warm.

For Roux: Melt butter in microwave. Blend in flour and cook on high for about 3 minutes until golden brown. Set aside.

For Gumbo: In a large skillet bring tomatoes and their juice to a boil. Add chicken, sausage, bay leaves and seasonings. Reduce heat, cover and simmer for 5 minutes. Add shrimp, green pepper and filé powder. Stir in roux. Cook until gumbo is thick and the shrimp are pink. Remove bay leaves. To serve, ladle gumbo into shallow soup plates and top with a serving of rice.
Serves 8

WHOLE CHICKEN-WHOLE DINNER

A full meal in one dish. To do it justice, the whole chicken must be used. The blend of flavors is absolutely delicious and will warm your soul.

1 chicken, about 3½ pounds
¼ cup olive oil
2 cloves garlic, peeled
1 bay leaf
3 to 4 lemon slices
1 teaspoon oregano

½ cup flour
2 onions, thickly sliced
6 to 8 small new potatoes, cut in half
1 cup chicken broth
¼ pound fresh green beans cut into 1 inch pieces
10 to 12 cherry tomatoes

Preheat oven to 375 degrees. Cut chicken into serving pieces, discarding back, wing tips and fat. Heat oil in a large skillet and cook garlic for 1 minute. Remove and place garlic in casserole with bay leaf, lemon slices and oregano. Salt and pepper chicken pieces, dust with flour and sauté in oil until browned. Add to casserole. Cook onions in the skillet for 2 minutes, adding more olive oil if needed. Drain and add to casserole with potatoes and chicken broth. Season with additional salt and pepper. Bake casserole uncovered for 30 minutes, basting twice. Cover. Bake another 20 to 30 minutes. Blanch beans in boiling salted water for 2 minutes. Drain and add to casserole with cherry tomatoes. Cover. Bake 5 to 10 minutes, or until done. Check seasonings and thicken gravy if desired.
Serves 6

CHICKEN HEKKA

Chicken Hekka is a classic island dish. In an old Maui cookbook, the German residents labeled this Scheiken Hecker. The word hekka will conjure up a dozen different dishes, as every cook uses a different combination of ingredients. Many happy memories of old time gatherings will doubtless come to mind, too. This is our recipe.

4 dried shiitake mushrooms, 4 inches in diameter
1 bundle long rice noodle, soaked and cut in half
1 pound boneless, skinless chicken thighs
1 tablespoon shoyu
4 tablespoons sake, divided
1 tablespoon oil

½ cup raw sugar
½ cup shoyu
1 large Kula onion, sliced
1 8-ounce can sliced bamboo shoots
2 cups watercress, cut into 2 inch pieces
4 green onions, cut diagonally into 2 inch lengths

Soak long rice and mushrooms separately in water about 1 hour. Cut the chicken into bite size pieces. Marinate in 1 tablespoon shoyu and 1 tablespoon sake. Drain mushrooms and discard stems, and slice caps. When ready to serve, heat l tablespoon oil in wok. When hot, stir-fry chicken for 2 to 3 minutes. Add sugar and stir-fry for 2 minutes Add remaining shoyu and sake. Stir.
Add mushrooms, bamboo shoots and long rice to wok. Stir.
Add the watercress and green onions and quickly heat through. Serve with rice.
Serves 6

KAHLUA TURKEY CHILI VERDE

"Chili and Rice" is a local staple, served at fairs, political rallies, pot lucks and family get togethers. Turkey thighs, Kahlua liqueur and fresh lime juice add a new and interesting twist.

3½ pounds turkey thighs
¼ cup olive oil
2 medium onions, chopped
12 large cloves garlic, peeled and chopped
1 large green bell pepper, chopped
2 tablespoons all purpose flour
1 28-ounce can Italian tomatoes,
   drained and chopped
1 13-ounce can tomatillos,
   drained and mashed

1 14-ounce can chicken broth
½ cup Kahlua
1½ cups chopped fresh cilantro
4 7-ounce cans diced mild green chilies
2 jalapeno chilies, diced
5 teaspoons dried oregano leaves
2 teaspoons ground coriander seeds
2 teaspoons ground cumin
Salt and freshly ground black pepper to taste
Lime wedges

KAHLUA TURKEY CHILI VERDE

In a large skillet brown the turkey thighs in olive oil over high heat, turning occasionally, for about 15 minutes. Transfer to a large roasting pan. Keep ¼ cup of the drippings in the skillet and add the onions, garlic and bell pepper.

Cook over medium heat until soft, about 10 minutes, stirring frequently.

Add flour, stir and cook 3 more minutes. Stir in the tomatoes, tomatillos, chicken broth, Kahlua, cilantro, green and jalapeno chilies, oregano, coriander and cumin.

Bring to a boil. Pour over turkey thighs in the roasting pan. Cover tightly with heavy foil and bake at 350 degrees for 1 hour. Remove from oven, loosen the foil and set pan aside to cool.

When cool enough to handle remove the skin and bones from the turkey. Cut the meat into half-inch cubes and place in a large pan with the sauce. Cook over medium heat until heated through. Season to taste with salt, pepper and fresh lime juice.

Pass bowls of various garnishes: grated Cheddar cheese, sour cream, chopped green onions, salsa, and additional wedges of fresh limes.

Serves 16

TURKEY SAUTÉ WITH WILD MUSHROOMS

The cultivation of wild mushrooms is turning into quite a big industry and they seem to be widely available now. It is an essential flavor in this recipe.

½ boneless, skinless turkey breast, about 1½ pounds
1 tablespoon juniper berries
2 cloves garlic
Salt and pepper
½ pound fresh wild mushrooms or ½ pound domestic plus 3 ounces dried wild mushrooms

1 cup crème fraîche or 1½ cup heavy cream
4 scallions, thinly sliced
2 tablespoons chopped parsley
4 tablespoons butter
¼ cup flour
½ cup chicken stock
1 teaspoon lemon juice

TURKEY SAUTÉ WITH WILD MUSHROOMS

Cut turkey into ½ inch thick slices then into 1 inch squares. Using a mortar and pestle or the back of a knife, crush together the juniper berries, garlic, 1 teaspoon salt and 1 teaspoon pepper until pulverized. Rub mixture into the turkey pieces and let stand for at least ½ hour. Slice the mushrooms. If using heavy cream, cook over medium heat until reduced to 1 cup (about 10 minutes). Set aside. Cut scallions into thin slices. Chop the parsley. All this can be done several hours ahead of time.

To cook: Melt the butter in a deep frying pan over medium heat. Dredge turkey in the flour, shake off excess and cook, working in batches if necessary, until golden brown (about 5 minutes per batch). Transfer turkey to a warm serving platter. Add mushrooms to the pan and cook until soft (about 4 minutes), add scallions and continue cooking 1 more minute. Stir in the chicken stock and crème fraîche or cream. Return turkey to pan. Cook until warmed through. Season the sauté with lemon juice, salt and pepper and garnish with chopped parsley.

Serves 4

TURKEY RAGOUT

This can be prepared ahead of time, refrigerated and reheated when you are ready to serve (always a blessing). It is attractive and has a nice mix of flavors.

¼ cup olive oil
⅓ cup flour
2 pounds turkey thighs, skinned, boned and
   cut into bite-size pieces (or substitute chicken
   thighs, but not breasts)
2 tablespoons minced fresh tarragon

2 large tomatoes, peeled, seeded and chopped
1 long strip orange zest
1 cup white wine
1 cup pitted green olives, halved
Salt and pepper to taste
2 tablespoons minced parsley

Heat oil in a large skillet over medium heat. Dredge the turkey in flour, shake off excess and sauté, cooking in batches if necessary, until golden brown, about 5 minutes per batch.
Stir in the tarragon, tomatoes, orange zest and wine. Cover and cook over very low heat, stirring occasionally and adding water if stew becomes too thick, until turkey is very tender, about 1 hour. Stir in the olives and season to taste with salt and pepper. Sprinkle with parsley and serve over rice.
Serves 6

FRESH TURKEY BREAST ALMONDINE

Crispy on the outside, moist on the inside. Everyone loves this!

1 cup whole natural almonds, toasted
6 turkey breast slices, about 1 pound
½ cup milk
2 eggs, beaten
½ cup flour
½ cup Italian seasoned dry bread crumbs

6 tablespoons butter
4 tablespoons vegetable oil
1 teaspoon garlic salt and fresh ground pepper
¾ cup fresh lemon juice
1 teaspoon sugar
2 tablespoons capers

Flatten turkey in waxed paper with mallet to ¼ inch thickness. Combine milk and eggs in a large glass bowl. Add turkey slices, coating well. Cover and refrigerate 2 to 3 hours or overnight. Coarsely chop ¼ cup almonds, set aside. Finely grind remaining almonds. Combine ground almonds with flour and bread crumbs. Coat turkey slices with the mixture. Cook the turkey in two batches. For each batch, heat 2 tablespoons each of butter and oil in a large skillet. Brown the turkey slices quickly, turning once. Add garlic salt and pepper to taste. Place on a heated serving platter and keep warm. If particles in pan are burning, wipe out pan before cooking the second batch. Stir lemon juice, sugar and remaining butter into pan. Boil for 2 minutes or until mixture thickens slightly. Add chopped almonds and capers. Spoon over turkey slices and serve.
Serves 6

CYNTHIA CONRAD

Plantation Days. Watercolor by Cynthia Conrad.

Plantation people visited almost daily over the hibiscus hedges that surrounded their small camp houses. Not everyone owned a car in those days. And besides that, gasoline cost money.

Sports teams provided recreation and healthy competition after work and on weekends. The men played baseball and basketball. In the evenings they went to the community hall or gym and learned *aikido* or *sumo* wrestling.

The checked palaka cloth from the plantation store was made up into sturdy shirts that offered protection from the sun and the sharp sugar cane and pineapple leaves.

Women made up bento lunches and placed them neatly into the tin cans their husbands, fathers and brothers took into the fields and the mills. There were balls of rice filled with salty, red plums called *ume,* slices of fried Spam and eggs fried like an omelet and eaten cold.

Was it really as simple a time as it seems in retrospect, a time of sharing and relying on each other. Or does it only seem that way from here?

VINHA D'ALHOS

Christmas wouldn't be the same in the Furtado home without this traditional Portuguese fare. Served with sweet bread hot from the oven, it is a hearty meal that Santa looks forward to every year.

4 pounds boneless pork butt, cut into 2" cubes
6 potatoes, peeled and cut in stew size chunks
6 carrots, peeled and cut in stew size chunks
Marinade:
  6 cloves garlic, minced
  1 tablespoon rock salt
  1 tablespoon brown sugar

2 Hawaiian red chili peppers, seeded
  and minced
1 cup cider vinegar
1 cup water
1 tablespoon black peppercorns
6 bay leaves, crushed
1 tablespoon vegetable oil

Combine ingredients for marinade. Add pork cubes and refrigerate overnight. Remove meat from marinade, reserving marinade. In a dutch oven, brown meat in 1 tablespoon of oil, over high heat. Add ¼ cup of reserved marinade, cover and simmer gently for 1½ hours, or until meat is tender. Add more liquid if necessary. In the remaining marinade, cook the potatoes and carrots until tender. When ready to serve, combine vegetables, meat and all the cooking liquid. Mix together and serve. Serves 6 to 8

PORK TENDERLOIN WITH ROSEMARY AND GARLIC

Pork tenderloin is almost comparable to chicken breasts in calories, cholesterol and fat which makes it a good choice for leaner cooking.

1½ to 2 pounds tenderloin of pork
2 tablespoons fresh rosemary, chopped
2 cloves garlic, minced

1 teaspoon salt
2 teaspoons coarse ground black pepper
2 tablespoons olive oil

Preheat oven to 400 degrees.
Chop rosemary, garlic, pepper and salt together in a food processor for 15 seconds. Pat all over the loin, pressing firmly onto the surface of the meat. Let it sit for 15 to 30 minutes. Using an oven-proof skillet, brown in the olive oil, until good and brown. Place skillet in oven and bake for exactly 20 minutes. Remove from oven and let rest for 5 minutes. The juices that collect in the skillet may be served au jus. Slice meat into thin slices and serve immediately.
Serves 4 to 6

CHINESE STYLE ROAST PORK

This needs to be marinated overnight for best results.

1½ pounds pork loin
⅓ cup shoyu
2 tablespoons medium dry sherry
2 tablespoons ketchup
1 tablespoon light brown sugar
2 tablespoons lemon juice
3 cloves garlic, minced
3 tablespoons fresh ginger, peeled and minced
Salt and pepper to taste

2 green onions
Chutney Garlic Sauce:
3 cloves garlic, minced
6 tablespoons shoyu
2 tablespoons red wine vinegar
½ cup mango chutney
2 tablespoons honey
1 teaspoon sesame oil
¼ cup water

Marinate pork in a combination of the first 9 ingredients for 3 hours or overnight, refrigerated. Preheat oven to 350 degrees. Reserve marinade. Roast pork on rack over ½" hot water in the bottom of roasting pan for 1¼ hours or until meat thermometer reads 155 degrees. Baste with reserved marinade. Let meat rest on warm platter for 5 minutes. Carve diagonally into thin slices. Sprinkle with green onion. Pass sauce separately.
Sauce: Combine garlic, shoyu and vinegar. Bring to a boil and simmer for 3 minutes. Add remaining sauce ingredients and bring to a boil again, stirring constantly.
Serves 6 to 8

PORK AND GREEN CHILI BURRITO

This makes a good meal for hearty young appetites either on the run as a burrito or as a family dinner served over rice.

3 pounds lean pork butt, cut into ¾ inch cubes
2 tablespoons vegetable oil
1 large onion, chopped
2 cloves garlic, minced
2 large green bell peppers, seeded and chopped
1 7-ounce can diced green chilies
1 teaspoon oregano
½ teaspoon ground cumin

1½ teaspoons salt
½ cup chopped fresh cilantro
1 tablespoon wine vinegar
¼ cup water
Warm flour tortillas
Coarsely chopped tomatoes
Sour cream
Lime wedges

Heat oil in Dutch oven and brown the pork. Pour off most of the fat and add the onion, garlic and green pepper. Sauté until limp. Add the chilies, oregano, cumin, salt, cilantro, vinegar and water. Cover and simmer until meat is tender, about 1 hour. To serve, spoon pork onto tortilla, top with tomato, sour cream and a squeeze of lime. Roll up and enjoy.
Serves 6 to 8

SWEET SOUR BEEF

This is more like an Island version of Southwest barbecue than the Chinese Sweet Sour Pork that might come to mind. It has been a family favorite in the Harders family for three generations.

5 pounds beef, cut in 2 inch cubes
2 teaspoons salt
½ teaspoon pepper
½ cup flour
3 onions, sliced
¾ cup hot water

½ cup brown sugar
2 tablespoons shoyu
¾ cup ketchup
2 tablespoons Worcestershire sauce
2 tablespoons vinegar

Preheat oven to 350 degrees.
Combine beef, salt, pepper and flour in a bag and shake until meat is well coated.
Empty bag into a greased casserole. Place onions on top of meat. Combine remaining ingredients and pour over meat and onions. Cover and bake for 2½ hours. Serve over rice.
Serves 10 to 12

BEEF PICCANTE

In the winter when the weather cools our tastes turn to heartier eating. This robust Italian fare lends itself to crisp evenings, a cozy fire, a bottle of red Chianti and good friends.

1 pound beef tenderloin, cut into 8 slices
16 ounces of linguine
1 pack Brown Gravy Mix 0.87 ounce (trust us.)
Juice of l lemon, plus enough water
    to measure 1 cup

¼ cup garlic butter
1 teaspoon red pepper flakes
½ cup chopped parsley
½ cup grated Parmesan cheese
Salt and pepper to taste

Cook linguine until al dente. Slice beef and set aside while you prepare the sauce. Prepare brown gravy according to package directions using the lemon and water mixture. Over high heat, quickly sauté slices of beef. Do not over cook. These should be served rare. Place pasta on a platter, top with slices of beef and pour gravy over all. Sprinkle with Parmesan cheese and chopped parsley.
Serves 4

BEER BRAISED BEEF

We love the sweet, tangy flavor of this beef and the wonderful aroma that fills our kitchen as it cooks.

3 pounds lean beef, chuck or rump
2 tablespoons oil, divided
6 cups sliced yellow onions
4 cloves garlic, mashed
Salt and pepper to taste
1 cup strong beef stock
2 to 3 cups beer

2 tablespoons brown sugar
Herb bouquet:
  6 sprigs parsley
  1 bay leaf
  ½ teaspoons thyme
1½ to 2 tablespoons cornstarch
2 tablespoons wine vinegar

Preheat oven to 325 degrees. Cut beef into slices 2 x 4 inches by ½ inch thick pieces. In a heavy skillet over high heat, brown beef, a few pieces at a time in half the oil. Set aside. Sauté the onions in remaining oil until lightly browned. Add garlic, salt and pepper. Remove from heat. In a fireproof, deep, 10"casserole alternately layer beef, onions, salt and pepper in two layers each. Heat beef stock in the browning skillet. Pour over the meat. Add enough beer to barely cover the meat. Add brown sugar, and herbs. Stir. Cover and bake for 2½ hours. Discard bay leaf and parsley. Drain cooking liquid. Skim off fat. Mix together cornstarch and vinegar. Stir into liquid and simmer for 3 to 5 minutes. Pour over meat. Serve with egg noodles or parslied potatoes.
Serves 8

ZELIE'S ROAST LAMB

Add a green salad, a crusty loaf of bread and a beautiful bottle of wine for a meal fit for a king.

1 5 to 6 pound leg of lamb
6 cloves garlic, peeled and cut into chips
2 teaspoons fresh or 1 teaspoon dried thyme
Sea salt and pepper to taste
2 pounds russet potatoes, peeled
  and very thinly sliced

2 large onions, peeled and very thinly sliced
5 medium tomatoes, cored and
  cut into thin horizontal slices
⅔ cup white wine
⅓ cup extra virgin olive oil

Preheat oven to 400 degrees.
Rub the bottom of a large oval porcelain gratin dish about 16"x10"x2" with garlic.
Divide the seasonings (garlic, thyme, salt and pepper) into three portions. Layer the potatoes in a single layer, and season with one portion of seasoning mix. Place a layer of sliced onions on top of this and season as with the potatoes. Layer the tomatoes on top of the onions and season with the last portion of the seasoning mix. Add the white wine, then the oil. Trim the thicker portions of fat from lamb. Season with salt and pepper. Place a sturdy cake or oven rack directly on top of the gratin dish. Set the lamb on the rack, allowing the juices to drip onto the vegetables. Roast uncovered about 1 hour and 30 minutes. Do not turn the lamb. Remove from the oven and allow to rest 20 minutes before serving. To serve, carve lamb into thin slices and arrange on warmed plates with vegetables alongside.
Serves 6 to 8

DIANA LEHR

Kula. Upcountry Ranch Land. Pastel by Diana Lehr.

Maui's great cattle ranches stretch across the face of Haleakala Crater, then wrap themselves seamlessly past Ulupalakua to Kaupo and Hana.
Ranch life in those remote, cooler regions has for generations been a part of Hawaiian life.
The special needs of the Hawaiian cowboy, or *paniolo*, have given birth to handcrafts unique to the islands - the *lauhala* cowboy hat with bands of peacock feathers or upcountry flowers, saddles, ropes and slack key guitars.
The paniolo, like cowboys everywhere, are a vanishing breed.
On afternoons during the winter months, rain squalls are seen moving quickly across the ranch lands, feeding thirsty *panini* and turning the pastures green almost overnight.

EASY OVEN CHOW MEIN

No time to stand over a hot wok? The name of this recipe says it all. Cut up the vegetables ahead of time, then assemble and bake the chow mein instead. It travels well for pot lucks, or expands well for large groups.

2 12-ounce packages fresh chow mein noodles
1½ cups thinly sliced carrots
1½ cups thinly sliced celery
1½ cups thinly sliced onion
1½ cups sliced green beans
1½ cups Chinese peas
1 10-ounce package mung bean sprouts
¾ cup thinly sliced char siu

2 tablespoons oyster sauce
2 tablespoons shoyu
¼ cup peanut oil
1 teaspoon garlic powder
1 egg, beaten, fried and cut into thin strips
1 tablespoon sesame seeds, toasted
3 green onions, chopped
¼ cup chopped cilantro

Preheat oven to 350 degrees.
Toss all ingredients, except egg, sesame seeds, green onion and cilantro and put in a large casserole. Cover and bake in oven for about 20 minutes, or until vegetables are cooked. Garnish with remaining ingredients and serve.
Serves 8 to 10

SAIMIN

Dickie's clean-out-the-refrigerator saimin. And who would know better?

Water and salt to cook noodles
6 cups of chicken, beef or vegetable broth
2 teaspoons shoyu
8 dried opae shrimp
4 ounces dry or uncooked saimin noodles per serving
Green onions, finely minced

Toppings:
Meat, fish, fowl, cut in thin strips such as:
roast pork, char siu, ham, steak, chicken, duck,
fish cake, shrimp
Vegetables, rough cut such as: choy sum, watercress,
bok choy, mustard cabbage, Chinese cabbage

Bring one gallon of water and 2 tablespoons of salt to a boil. Cook the noodles for three minutes or until tender. Do not overcook. Drain. Rinse with cold water and set aside. Blanch vegetables and rinse with cold water. Place noodles in individual bowls. Cover with choice of meats and vegetables. Bring broth to a high boil and pour over noodles and toppings. Garnish with green onions.
Serves 4 to 6

CHOW FUN

Everyone loves noodles, it seems. Sold in a paper cone with wooden chopsticks at every Island fair... Maui's answer to the hot dog.

2-7ounce packages chow fun noodles,
    cooked and drained
1 tablespoon cooking oil
2 teaspoons minced fresh ginger
2 cloves of garlic, minced
½ pound of ground pork
4 tablespoons shoyu, divided

1 cup grated carrot
1 cup sliced green beans
1 cup mung bean sprouts
1 tablespoon sesame oil
½ cup chopped green onions
1 tablespoon oyster sauce

In a large skillet, heat the oil and quickly stir in ginger and garlic, cooking until fragrant. Add pork and brown, stirring as it cooks. When it is browned, season with 2 tablespoons shoyu.
Add the carrots and sliced beans. Stir together until just crisp-cooked. Add the mung bean sprouts and cook for 30 seconds. Add the noodles, toss with the meat and vegetables until well blended.
Add the sesame oil, 2 more tablespoons of shoyu and the oyster sauce.
Toss again and heat until noodles are hot, all the vegetables are cooked and flavors are blended. Top with chopped green onions. Add more shoyu if desired.
Serves 6

PANCIT

The popular Filipino noodles found at most celebrations and fairs are enjoyed by everyone.

1 7½-ounce package long rice
6 dried shiitake mushrooms
¼ pound shrimp
4 cloves garlic, minced
½ pound ground pork
1 medium carrot, cut into matchstick pieces
¼ head cabbage, chopped

2 tablespoons vegetable oil
3 cups chicken broth
3 tablespoon patis (fish sauce)
½ teaspoon pepper
1 teaspoon salt
1 8-ounce package pancit canton or chuka soba
4 green onions, thinly sliced

Soak long rice in water ½ hour, drain and cut into 3 inch lengths. Soak shiitake mushrooms in water until soft, drain and squeeze dry, discard stems, and slice thinly. Clean shrimp and cut into small pieces. Heat vegetable oil in wok and quickly sauté garlic and brown pork. Add carrots, shrimp,and cabbage, stir-frying about 2 minutes. Add chicken broth, patis, pepper and salt and bring to a boil. Add long rice, mushrooms and then noodles, stirring for a few minutes until noodles are softened and cooked. Top with green onions.
Serves 6

SHRIMP AND CAKE NOODLES

This is a pretty dish to serve, delicious to eat and easy to prepare if you just follow the steps as they are laid out below. Allow yourself about one and a quarter hours to make.

l pound large 16 to 20 shrimp
2 tablespoons oil
2 teaspoons shoyu
2 cloves of garlic, minced, divided
1 teaspoon grated fresh ginger
2 6-ounce packages Chuka Soba noodles
2 tablespoons sesame oil
1 medium stalk broccoli, peeled and sliced
½ Kula onion, sliced in thin wedges
2 stalks celery, sliced on diagonal

½ red pepper sliced in ¼ inch strips
1 small carrot cut in matchstick pieces
¼ pound mushrooms, sliced
Sauce:
1½ tablespoons cornstarch
½ teaspoon garlic powder
1 heaping teaspoon grated fresh ginger
1 tablespoon shoyu
1 cup chicken broth

SHRIMP AND CAKE NOODLES

Clean shrimp and marinate in oil, shoyu, garlic and ginger for 1 hour in the refrigerator.

Cook noodles, drain and toss with sesame oil. Spread in a 9"x 13" baking pan.

Spray top of noodles with vegetable oil.

Preheat broiler. Broil as close to heat as possible for 5 minutes or until crisp.

Invert noodle cake onto oiled baking sheet, spray with oil and broil 5 minutes more.

Turn off broiler, close oven door and leave noodles in oven to keep warm.

Heat wok and spray with oil. Drain shrimp and quickly cook until pink.

Remove shrimp and put on a plate. Combine sauce ingredients.

Stir fry vegetables 1 minute. Add ¼ cup water, cover and steam 1 minute.

Uncover, add sauce and stir until sauce thickens. Add shrimp and serve over cake noodles.

Serves 6

MACARIO PASCUAL

Morning at Cut Mountain. Shore Fishing. Oil by Macario Pascual.

Perhaps the quiet time near the ocean is where the real magic of shore fishing lies. The process of laying the lines and securing the rods in the sand and between the rocks has always seemed so solitary, almost meditative.

Those who shore fish, do it regularly. They pack up their jeeps, vans and rusty secondhand cars- vehicles that can take the salt and the abuse of the shore. Once there, out comes the gear, the coolers, hibachi, bright blue tarps and the bait-often frozen in plastic bags. There used to be the black, red and white hanafuda cards, too. Now more than likely a stack of regular playing cards will be accompanied by a boom box and tapes.

Does it matter if any fish are actually caught? Probably so. But more than anything, it's the break from the routine of the week, the sound of the ocean and the smell and feel of the *ehukai.*

SESAME RICE WITH LIME

The rice can cook in the oven or rice cooker while you prepare the rest of the meal. Add the seasonings just before you are ready to serve.

1½ cups brown rice
3½ cups broth
1 tablespoon oil
¼ cup coarsely chopped pecans
¼ cup sesame seeds

A pinch of thyme
A pinch of cayenne pepper
Salt and pepper to taste
2 limes cut into wedges

Preheat oven to 350 degrees.
Put rice and broth in a tightly covered casserole and cook for an hour, or cook in rice cooker. You get the best results if you soak the rice for several hours before cooking. When rice is cooked, heat a skillet over medium heat and add l tablespoon of oil. Sauté pecans until slightly brown. Set aside. In the same pan toast sesame seeds until brown. Add the thyme and cayenne and cook briefly, stirring so they do not burn. When rice is done, stir in seasonings and serve a portion, giving each person a wedge of lime to squeeze over the top of the rice if desired.
Serves 6 to 8

STEAMED BROCCOLI WITH CHINESE MUSHROOMS

A unique and pretty dinner party vegetable with an Asian accent.

10 dried Chinese black mushrooms or
   dried shiitake
1 teaspoon sesame oil
1½ pounds broccoli

3 tablespoons vegetable oil
2 large cloves garlic, chopped
¼ cup oyster sauce
3 tablespoons chicken broth

Soak mushrooms in 1½ cups hot water for 30 minutes. Drain, discard the stems and cut the caps in half. Arrange caps on a heat proof plate and sprinkle with sesame oil, turning to coat evenly. Place plate on a rack set over boiling water, cover and steam for 15 minutes. Set aside.
Cut broccoli into 2 inch florets. Peel stalks and cut into 2 inch pieces. Mound the broccoli on a rack and steam, covered, over boiling water for 4 to 6 minutes, until bright green and just tender.
Transfer the broccoli to a platter, arranging it in a bundle shape, and keep warm. Heat a wok over moderately high heat. Add the vegetable oil and garlic and stir fry until the garlic is golden. Add the mushroom caps and stir fry for one minute. Reduce heat to moderate low and add the combined oyster sauce and chicken broth. Bring the sauce to a simmer and spoon it over the broccoli.
Serves 4

ROASTED ROSEMARY POTATOES

The rosemary-steeped butter is the secret to these potatoes and must be done ahead of time. Allow enough time for this recipe and you will be well rewarded.

¼ cup butter
1 teaspoon dried rosemary or sprig of fresh
4 to 5 medium white potatoes
Hawaiian rock salt

Melt the butter and add the rosemary. Let the mixture sit at room temperature for at least 2 hours. Preheat oven to 450 degrees.
Cut the potatoes in ¼ inch slices. Place on a lightly buttered baking sheet in a slightly overlapping pattern. Drizzle butter and rosemary over potatoes and sprinkle with rock salt. Bake for 20 minutes, or until tender and crispy.
Serves 6

LEMON WALNUT BROCCOLI

Even non-broccoli-lovers have exclaimed about this preparation. Of course conventional methods can be used as well, but the microwave makes preparation a snap.

1½ pounds broccoli, separated into ¾ " florets,
    the stems peeled and cut crosswise ¼ " thick
3 tablespoons butter
2 tablespoons walnuts, minced

1 tablespoon dry bread crumbs
1½ teaspoons freshly minced lemon zest

In a shallow microwave-safe baking dish, combine the broccoli with 2 tablespoons water.
Cover with plastic wrap and microwave on high for 3 minutes or until tender.
Pour off any liquid, toss with butter, sprinkle with walnuts, breadcrumbs and lemon zest.
Toss again. Microwave, uncovered, on high for 1½ minutes or until heated through.
Serves 6

CHINESE PEAS WITH SHIITAKE MUSHROOMS

Hardly a day goes by that one of us doesn't have a quick stir-fry vegetable for dinner. We think this is a winner.

6 dried shiitake mushrooms
2 tablespoons peanut oil
½ cup shredded bamboo shoots

1 pound Chinese peas
1½ teaspoons salt
1 teaspoon sugar

In a small bowl cover mushrooms with ½ cup warm water and let soak for 30 minutes. Reserve 2 tablespoons of the soaking water, then drain mushrooms, discard stems and cut caps into quarters. Set wok or 10-inch skillet over high heat for 30 seconds. Add oil, and heat for an additional 30 seconds. Immediately drop in mushrooms and bamboo shoots and stir-fry for 2 minutes. Add Chinese peas, salt, sugar and the reserved mushroom soaking liquid. Cook, stirring constantly, over high heat for about 2 minutes, or until the water evaporates. Transfer to a heated platter and serve at once.
Serves 6 to 8

DEVO'S BEANS

Devo is a Seattle restaurateur who, on a Maui visit, whipped up these beans, as part of a memorable barbecue for a few of his friends. He gave this recipe to Rosemary, his hostess, on condition that she guard it with her life - which she did, until Devo gave her permission to share with you.

2 onions, chopped
1 pound Portuguese sausage, chopped
2 28-ounce cans B & B baked beans
2 16-ounce cans lima beans, drained
2 16-ounce cans garbanzo beans, drained

2 16-ounce cans black eyed peas, drained
1 14-ounce bottle catsup (1¾ cups)
3½ ounces French's prepared mustard (⅓ cup)
1 cup brown sugar
2 to 3 tablespoons Liquid Smoke

Sauté onion and Portuguese sausage. Combine all ingredients and pour into a large casserole. Cover and bake at 250 degrees for 1½ hours.
Serves 20

BLACK BEAN CHILI

A crowd pleaser, this hearty vegetarian main dish can be made ahead - even frozen. You might want to reduce the amount of jalapeno chilies although for some reason, the "fire" is reduced if the dish sits for a day before serving.

4 cups black beans, dry
2 tablespoons cumin seed
2 tablespoons dried oregano leaves
2 large onions, finely chopped
1½ cups finely chopped green bell peppers
2 cloves garlic, minced
½ cup olive oil
1 teaspoon cayenne pepper
1½ tablespoons paprika

1 teaspoon salt
3 cups canned crushed whole tomatoes
½ cup finely chopped jalapeno chilies
   (canned okay)
½ pound Jack or Cheddar cheese, grated
½ cup green onions, finely chopped
⅔ cup sour cream
8 sprigs of cilantro

BLACK BEAN CHILI

Sort through the beans and remove any small pebbles. Rinse beans well.

Place in a large pot and cover with water to several inches above top of beans.

Cover and bring to a boil.

Reduce heat and cook until tender, about 1½ hours, adding more water as necessary.

Drain, reserving one cup of liquid. Return this one cup to the beans.

Cook cumin seed and the oregano in a small pan in a 325 degree oven for 10 minutes until fragrant.

Sauté onions, green peppers and garlic in oil with the cumin seed, oregano, cayenne pepper, paprika and salt for 10 minutes, or until the onions are soft.

Mix in tomatoes and chilies and add to the beans. Stir well. At this point the chili can be refrigerated.

When ready to serve, heat thoroughly.

To serve: Put grated cheese in the bottom of a chili bowl. Add hot chili.

Top with a spoonful of sour cream, a sprinkle of green onion, and a sprig of cilantro.

Serves 10 to 12

HERBED LENTIL CASSEROLE

This is a satisfying vegetarian entrée It is also wonderful as a side dish with grilled or roasted meat. A large link of sausage cooked on the grill is particularly delicious as an accompaniment.

¾ cup lentils
½ cup brown rice
1 cup water
1 cup chicken broth
1 medium onion, chopped
1¼ cups dry white wine

½ teaspoon dried basil leaves
¼ teaspoon dried thyme leaves
½ teaspoon salt
¼ teaspoon garlic powder
3 tablespoons Mozzarella
   or Cheddar cheese, grated

Preheat oven to 350 degrees.
Butter casserole. Combine all ingredients except cheese in a 1½ quart casserole. Bake uncovered for about 1½ hours until moist but not runny. Sprinkle cheese on top and bake an additional 5 minutes.
Serves 6 to 8

GREEN BEANS WITH BASIL

Our all-time favorite way of fixing beans.

½ pound red ripe tomatoes
¾ pound fresh green beans, stemmed
    and cut into 2" pieces
3 tablespoons olive oil

2 teaspoons finely minced garlic
2 tablespoons finely chopped fresh basil
Salt and pepper to taste

Cut tomatoes crosswise in half, squeeze out seeds, and cut into ¼"cubes. There should be 1 cup.
Steam green beans until just tender. Heat oil in skillet, add garlic and cook briefly, without browning.
Add tomatoes, salt and pepper and cook for 30 seconds, stirring constantly. Add beans and basil.
Toss to blend and cook 30 seconds more.
Serves 4

ZUCCHINI CASSEROLE

For summer dining - when you are drowning in zucchini!

8 cups diced zucchini
1 medium green bell pepper,
  chopped fine
1 medium onion, chopped fine
1 cup stale white bread crumbs
1 cup grated sharp Cheddar cheese

½ cup olive oil
1 tablespoon minced fresh basil or
  1 teaspoon dried basil
2 large eggs, beaten well
1 teaspoon salt
¼ teaspoon pepper

Preheat oven to 350 degrees.
In a bowl combine the zucchini, green pepper, onion, bread crumbs, cheese, oil, basil, eggs,
salt and pepper. Transfer to a 1½ quart baking dish, cover with foil.
Bake in oven for 45 minutes.
Remove foil and continue to cook until the top is lightly browned.
Serves 6 to 8

CHEESY GARLIC GRITS

~~~~~~

A particularly delicious version of a standard recipe, and one which we serve all the time. Our vegetarian friends make a whole meal of it.

4 cups water
1 cup white hominy quick grits
1½ cups grated sharp Cheddar cheese
½ cup butter

½ cup milk
2 large eggs, well beaten
1 small clove garlic, minced
Salt and pepper to taste

Preheat oven to 350 degrees.
Butter a 2 quart casserole and set aside.
Bring water to a boil and slowly stir in the grits. Reduce heat to medium-low, cover and cook for 5 minutes, stirring occasionally, until thickened. Remove from heat and stir in butter and cheese.
Add milk, eggs and garlic, stir, and pour into casserole. Bake uncovered for l hour or until top is set and lightly puffed.
Serves 6 to 8

AUNT LOU'S CORN CASSEROLE

On Thanksgiving Day, this is a must for all of the Furtados. Even when we can't be together, Aunt Lou's corn casserole is on all our tables. Rich, but well worth the calories!

2 10-ounce packages frozen corn
3 eggs
3 tablespoons sugar

Salt and pepper
1½ pints whipping cream
1 tablespoon butter

Preheat oven to 350 degrees.
Thaw corn and put into a buttered shallow casserole dish. Beat together eggs, sugar, salt and pepper. Add the cream and beat briefly, just to combine. Pour over corn, dot with remaining butter and bake uncovered for 50 to 60 minutes or until set.
Serves 6 to 8

JULIENNE OF VEGETABLES

A beautiful presentation and a lovely fresh taste. The trick is to cook the vegetables quickly and separately so they maintain their own character, combining them only at the last minute.

1 carrot, peeled
1 small zucchini
1 small crookneck squash
½ red bell pepper
½ Kula onion, sliced

¼ pound mushrooms, sliced
2-3 tablespoons butter
1 tablespoon chopped fresh basil
1 teaspoon sugar
1 teaspoon salt

Julienne carrot, zucchini, crookneck squash and red bell pepper. Set aside in separate piles.
In a wok or large frying pan, over high heat, quickly sauté each vegetable separately, using a little butter for each batch, until crisp cooked. Do not overcrowd the pan. Return all the vegetables to the pan and toss quickly with seasonings and serve immediately.
Serves 4

SCOTT BURNS

Makawao Rodeo, Fourth of July. Flying Weenies. Watercolor by Scott Burns.

The bleachers groan from the weight of the crowd, as a sheer cloud of brown dirt from the rodeo ring rains down on happy 4th of July revelers. It's the Makawao Rodeo, a mid-summer tradition held on the outskirts of this small upcountry town.

The ramshackle storefronts were witness earlier to a parade - the kind only a small town can throw - and now everyone and his cousin is downing hot dogs spilling over with relish, and hamburgers. It's the usual 4th of July fare.

Only in Makawao, to the beer and the sodas, you have to add paper bowls steaming with spicy Portuguese soup, followed by sweet, hot malasadas - a yeasty doughnut fried in hot oil and covered with sugar before being dropped by the dozen into brown paper bags that soak up the grease.

It's an outdoor cookout. A family event. A place to see and be seen. Never mind the rodeo, it's just a reason to be out in the fresh air, and to catch up on the local gossip with people you rarely see anymore. A reason not to cook. A time to celebrate living on Maui.

PINEAPPLE COFFEE BREAD

It disappears as fast as we can make it.

½ teaspoon cinnamon
5 tablespoons sugar
2 cups sugar
1 cup shortening
2½ cups crushed pineapple
    (20 ounce can, undrained)

4 eggs, well beaten
3 cups cake flour
1 teaspoon salt
2 teaspoons baking soda
2 teaspoons baking powder

Preheat oven to 350 degrees.
Grease 2 five by nine inch loaf pans. Line with waxed paper and grease again.
Mix together 5 tablespoons sugar and ½ teaspoon cinnamon and set aside.
Cream sugar and shortening in a large bowl until light and fluffy. Add pineapple and eggs.
Sift together flour, salt, baking soda and baking powder *three* times. Add to pineapple mixture, stirring
lightly until *just* blended. Pour batter into the prepared pans and sprinkle with cinnamon sugar mix.
Bake for 50 to 60 minutes, or until it they test done. Texture and flavor improve if allowed to rest overnight.
Serves 10

GINI'S MOM'S CINNAMON ROLLS

The easiest cinnamon rolls we have ever made!

3 scant cups flour
¼ cup sugar
½ teaspoon salt
1 cup water, divided
½ cup margarine or butter
1 egg
1 tablespoon granular yeast

2 to 3 tablespoons butter
½ cup raisins
¼ cup brown sugar
1 tablespoon cinnamon
2 cups powdered sugar
3 to 4 tablespoons boiling water

Sift together flour, sugar and salt into large mixing bowl. Combine ½ cup of the water and the margarine in a small saucepan and heat until margarine is melted. Add to flour mixture.
Beat the egg and add to the remaining ½ cup of water, sprinkle with yeast and beat into the flour mixture until smooth. Cover bowl and place in refrigerator for at least 4 hours or overnight.
Preheat oven to 350 degrees.
Roll the dough out on a floured board to a 10 x 12 inch rectangle about ½ inch thick. Dot with butter and sprinkle with raisins, sugar and cinnamon. Roll lengthwise like a jelly roll and cut into 12 one inch slices. Place on a greased 9 x 13 x 2 inch pan, cut side down, and let rise at room temperature for about l hour. Bake for 25 minutes, or until done. Combine powdered sugar and boiling water and spoon over the hot rolls.
Yields 12 rolls

SOUR CREAM MUFFINS

It is important to use only sweetened and toasted wheat germ for these muffins.

½ cup shortening
1 cup brown sugar
2 eggs
1 cup flour, sifted
½ teaspoon salt

1 teaspoon baking powder
1 teaspoon baking soda
1 cup sour cream
1 cup Honey Crunch wheat germ

Preheat oven to 400 degrees.
Cream shortening and sugar in a large mixing bowl. Beat in eggs. Sift together flour, salt, baking powder and baking soda. Add dry ingredients to the egg mixture alternately with the sour cream. Fold in wheat germ. Fill greased or paper lined muffin tins ⅔ full.
Bake for 15 to 20 minutes.
Yields 18 muffins

APPLE THYME COFFEE CAKE

This recipe was given to our designer who lives in San Francisco - with an apple tree in her back yard and a bed of thyme at her kitchen door. It is best served right out of the oven.

½ cup softened butter
¾ cup sugar
2 eggs
1½ cups cake flour
½ cup white corn meal
2 teaspoons baking powder

½ teaspoon baking soda
¼ teaspoon salt
½ cup buttermilk
2 cups peeled and chopped apples
2 tablespoons fresh, crumbled thyme leaves

Preheat oven to 350 degrees.
Cream butter and sugar in a large bowl. Add eggs and beat until blended. In another bowl, combine cake flour, corn meal, baking powder, baking soda and salt. Sift together and set aside.
Beat buttermilk into egg, sugar and butter mixture, then add the sifted dry ingredients and beat until smooth. Add apples and thyme and blend well. Pour into a greased and floured 8 x 8 inch pan and bake for 45 minutes, or until a toothpick inserted into the center of the cake comes out clean.
Serves 9

FRENCH DOUGHNUT MUFFINS

These delicious morsels have the flavor of a cake doughnut but not the fat.

1½ cups flour
1 cup sugar, divided
2 teaspoons baking powder
¼ teaspoon salt
¼ teaspoon nutmeg
½ cup milk

1 egg, beaten
⅓ cup melted butter or margarine
½ teaspoon vanilla extract
1 teaspoon cinnamon
Melted butter

Preheat oven to 400 degrees.
Sift flour with ½ cup of the sugar, baking powder, salt and nutmeg into a large mixing bowl.
Combine milk, egg, melted butter and vanilla and add to flour mixture, stirring only until ingredients are moistened.
Fill greased muffin tins half full and bake 20 minutes. Remove from pan, immediately brush with melted butter and roll in remaining ½ cup of sugar mixed with cinnamon.
Yields 12 muffins

BUTTERMILK SCONE

Sometimes it is nice to have a recipe that makes a small amount of bread. This goes together quickly, tastes delicious and is a great addition to a Sunday morning breakfast for two.

1 cup flour
1½ tablespoons sugar
1 teaspoon baking powder
⅛ teaspoon baking soda
¼ cup cold butter cut into small pieces

½ teaspoon grated orange peel
2 tablespoons currants
¼ cup buttermilk
⅛ teaspoon ground cinnamon
2 teaspoons sugar

Preheat oven to 375 degrees.
In a medium bowl combine flour, sugar, baking powder and baking soda. Add butter, rubbing with fingers to form fine crumbs. Stir in orange peel and currants.
Make a well in the center and add buttermilk. Stir with fork until dough holds together. Pat dough into ball and knead on a floured board 5 or 6 turns. Shape dough into smooth ball and place in a greased 9 inch cake pan.
Mix cinnamon and sugar and sprinkle on ball of dough. Bake for 10 minutes. With a sharp knife cut an "X" ½ inch deep across the top. Continue baking until golden brown, about 25 minutes more.
Serve warm from the oven.
Serves 2

CHOCOLATE BREAD

Use your bread machine, if you have a large one. Hot bread will be waiting for you for breakfast. We've given conventional methods - which, of course, work just fine.

l cup milk
2 tablespoons butter
½ cup sugar
1 teaspoon vanilla
1 package yeast

1 tablespoon sugar
2 eggs, beaten
3½ cups flour
⅔ cup sifted unsweetened cocoa
Hawaiian raw sugar (optional)

In a small saucepan scald the milk, remove from heat and add butter, sugar and vanilla. In a separate small bowl dissolve the yeast in ¼ cup tepid water. Stir in sugar. When the milk has cooled slightly add the yeast mixture and the beaten eggs. Stir well. Mix flour and cocoa in a large bowl. Make a well in the flour and pour in the liquid. Mix well and turn out onto a floured board. Let dough rest for 10 minutes. Knead dough about 5 minutes, adding flour as necessary.
Place dough in a clean, buttered bowl, cover with a dry cloth and let rise until doubled, about ½ hour. Punch down dough and knead 8 to 10 times. Pat and shape into loaf. Place seam side down in a 9 x 5 inch buttered loaf pan. Cover and let rise to top of pan, about 45 minutes. Preheat oven to 350 degrees, sprinkle with Hawaiian raw sugar and bake for l hour on middle rack of oven. After 30 minutes cover loaf with foil to prevent top from burning. Let cool 10 minutes. Turn out onto wire rack and serve warm with vanilla butter.

VANILLA BUTTER

This vanilla butter is the natural partner to the chocolate bread on the preceding page. This butter and bread are perfect with breakfast Kona coffee, afternoon tea, dessert or a snack anytime.

12 tablespoons butter
¾ cup confectioners sugar
2 tablespoons vanilla extract

Beat all ingredients together until well blended and fluffy.
Spread liberally on slices of warm chocolate bread.

JAN KASPRZYCKI

Keanae Taro. Taro Patches. Oil by Jan Kasprzycki.

Taro patches once wove their block patterns on the floors of valleys all over Hawaii. The *kalo* was a food staple - its lore stretched back to the beginnings of the people - it was their connection to the earth. Work in the taro patches has always been hard and dirty, but never demeaning. It was work for the whole family - happy work for the good of the *ohana*. Something done by your ancestors for as far back as anyone could remember, and now done by you too.

Taro, pounded into *poi,* steamed or fried and eaten with butter or coconut milk, was sustenance. Farmers worked the land for themselves and for their *ali'i.*

There are fewer taro patches in rural Hawaii. It's hard to get anyone to work that hard in the water and mud. Still, there are a few young people who believe in the taro and life on the land. They come back from places like Honolulu and Los Angeles to try to make a difference-to keep the *kalo* culture alive.

OVER THE TOP COOKIES

A family favorite for four generations! The original recipe came from a community cookbook published fifty years ago.

½ cup butter
1 cup sugar
2 eggs, separated
1½ cups pastry flour
1 teaspoon baking powder

Pinch of salt
1 teaspoon vanilla
1 cup brown sugar
1 cup chopped walnuts

Preheat oven to 350 degrees.
Mix together the butter, sugar, egg yolks, flour, baking powder, salt and vanilla. Press into an 8-inch buttered pan and bake for 15 minutes. Beat egg whites until stiff, adding brown sugar a bit at a time. Fold in nuts, and spread mixture on baked crust.
Return pan to oven and bake an additional 25 minutes.
Yields 16

COCONUT SHORTBREAD COOKIES

The sugar plantations employed people from all over the world. The Scots brought their traditional shortbread. We added coconut.

8 ounces unsalted butter
1 cup sugar
2 cups sifted flour-sift before measuring
1 teaspoon salt
1½ cups shredded coconut

Preheat oven to 300 degrees.
Cream the butter with the sugar. Sift together the flour and salt and add to the butter and sugar mixture. Sir in the coconut and blend well. Shape the dough into 2 rolls and wrap in wax paper. Refrigerate until firm. Cut into ¼ inch thick slices.
Bake for 20 minutes, or until lightly browned.
Yields 8 dozen

BREAKFAST COOKIES

Cookies for breakfast? Why not! Not too sweet, a basket full of these set out at a B & B, or at home would make a welcome snack at any time of the day.

2 cups quick cooking oats
2 cups flour
½ teaspoon salt
½ teaspoon baking soda

1 cup light brown sugar
2 tablespoons sesame seeds, toasted
3 tablespoons hot water
1 cup butter, melted

Preheat oven to 350 degrees.
In a large mixing bowl, combine oats, flour, salt, baking soda, sugar and sesame seeds. Add hot water and melted butter, mix thoroughly and form into 1 inch balls. Place on an ungreased cookie sheet and flatten each with a fork. Bake about 10 minutes, or until brown. Immediately transfer cookies from baking sheet to a wire rack to cool.
Yields 6 dozen

BROWNIES SUPREME

Sometimes a plain brownie doesn't seem special enough. These double frosted morsels are wonderful served with sliced fruit for dessert, next to a big pot of coffee at a cocktail party or even as part of a buffet. Of course they are equally good eaten at the kitchen table with a glass of milk!

2 ounces unsweetened chocolate, divided
¾ cup butter, divided into thirds
1 egg
½ cup sugar
¼ cup flour

1 cup chopped pecans or walnuts
2 cups unsifted confectioners sugar
2-3 tablespoons whipping cream
½ teaspoon vanilla

Preheat oven to 350 degrees.
Melt one ounce of the chocolate with ¼ cup of the butter.
In a small bowl beat together the egg and sugar. Slowly beat in the melted chocolate and butter mix. Stir in flour and nuts with a spoon (not a beater) and spread in lightly greased 9 inch square baking pan. Bake for 20 minutes. Cool.
Cream ¼ cup of the butter, the confectioners sugar, the cream and vanilla together and spread over cooled brownies. Melt the second ounce of chocolate and the remaining ¼ cup butter together and drizzle over the cream frosting, tilting the pan so chocolate covers evenly. Chill 10 minutes.
Cut into squares.
Yields 25

CHINESE ALMOND COOKIES

Just like those we have enjoyed in Chinese restaurants. A perfect way to end a light stir-fry meal.

2 cups flour
½ teaspoon soda
¾ teaspoon baking powder
1 egg
½ pound lard (the secret ingredient)

½ cup granulated sugar
½ cup brown sugar, packed
1 to 2 teaspoons almond extract
Whole blanched almonds
1 or 2 egg yolks

Preheat oven to 350 degrees.
Sift flour with soda and baking powder. Beat egg and lard together. Add sugars and almond extract. Gradually mix in dry ingredients until well blended. For each cookie, roll 1 tablespoon dough to make a ball. Place on ungreased baking sheet and press an almond into the middle. Brush top with beaten egg yolk and bake for 15 to 20 minutes.
Yields 36

CHEWY CHRISTMAS COOKIES

The combination of citron, lemon and brown sugar results in a sweet, tart cookie. The citron is a taste of the holidays as it is the only time it is available on Maui.

2 cups brown sugar
½ cup honey
1 lemon grated and juiced
1 orange grated
¼ cup butter
2 tablespoons milk
1 egg, beaten

2½ cups flour
1 tablespoon baking powder
1 teaspoon cinnamon
½ teaspoon salt
½ teaspoon ground cloves
⅛ teaspoon nutmeg
½ cup chopped citron

Preheat oven to 350 degrees.
Put sugar, honey, lemon juice and rind, and orange rind into a saucepan over low heat and stir, cooking until sugar is dissolved. Do not boil. Add butter and stir. Set aside to cool. When cool, add milk, egg, flour, baking powder, cinnamon, salt, cloves and nutmeg. Mix well. Chop citron with a bit of flour. Add to batter. Drop batter by teaspoons onto buttered cookie sheets and bake for 8 to 10 minutes. Remove cookies from pan immediately and place on wire racks to cool.
Yields 9 dozen

GINGER CRINKLE COOKIES

If you are not a baker this recipe is for you! It always works. It is very easy. We love the sugary, crinkled top and the taste of ginger.

2 cups flour
2 teaspoons baking soda
1 teaspoon cinnamon
1 teaspoon cloves
1 teaspoon ground ginger

¼ teaspoon salt
1⅓ cups sugar, divided
¾ cup shortening (not butter) softened
¼ cup light molasses
1 egg

Preheat oven to 375 degrees.
Sift flour with baking soda, cinnamon, cloves, ginger and salt. Set aside.
In large bowl of electric mixer, at medium speed, gradually add 1 cup of the sugar to the softened shortening, creaming until very light and fluffy about 5 minutes.
Blend in molasses and egg. At low speed, beat in flour mixture until just blended. Refrigerate one hour. Shape dough into 1¼ inch balls, roll in remaining sugar, and place 2 inches apart on a greased cookie sheet. Bake for 8 to 10 minutes. Remove to wire rack to cool.
Yields 3 dozen

PEANUT BUTTER SQUARES

The better the ingredients, the better the final product, so use real butter, high quality peanut butter and real chocolate chips.

1½ cups graham cracker crumbs (22 squares)
1 pound confectioners sugar
½ pound butter, melted

1 cup creamy peanut butter
12 ounces chocolate chips

Mix crumbs and sugar in food processor. Add butter and peanut butter and mix well. Press into a 9 x 13 x 2 inch baking pan, cover with waxed paper, smooth the surface and chill for 20 minutes. Remove waxed paper. Melt chocolate chips over very low heat, stirring until smooth. Pour over peanut butter crust, smooth with a rubber spatula and cool until the chocolate is set. Cut into squares and serve, or package in a plastic wrapping and store in refrigerator or freezer. It is best served at room temperature. It *must* be at room temperature to cut into squares.
Yields about 40

PINE TREE SHILLINGS

In the early days of our country, one of the coins of the realm was a copper shilling with the image of a pine tree on it. If you use a cookie press with a pine tree design, or draw a pine tree with a toothpick, these small crisp molasses cookies might remind you of the early "Pine Tree Shillings" as these coins were called.

½ cup butter
l cup light molasses
½ cup light brown sugar
3 cups flour

½ teaspoon baking soda
½ teaspoon salt
½ teaspoon ground ginger
½ teaspoon cinnamon

Preheat oven to 350 degrees.
In a medium sauce pan heat and blend together the butter, molasses and brown sugar.
Remove from heat and cool. Sift together dry ingredients, add to cooled butter mixture and beat well. Roll dough into balls the size of a small marble and place on a greased cookie sheet. Flatten with the bottom of a glass dipped either into water or sugar. Cookies should be about 2 inches in diameter. Bake for 8 to 10 minutes.
Makes about 100 cookies.

PINEAPPLE ALMOND BARS

These bars stay fresh and moist for a long time. They also freeze very well.

2 cups flour
2 cups firmly packed brown sugar
½ cup butter, softened
1 cup coarsely chopped toasted almonds
1 teaspoon cinnamon
1 teaspoon baking soda

½ teaspoon salt
1 egg
¾ cup sour cream
1 teaspoon vanilla
½ cup drained crushed pineapple
Confectioners sugar

Preheat oven to 350 degrees.
In a medium bowl, mix flour, sugar and butter until crumbled. Stir in almonds. Measure 2 cups of this mixture and press onto the bottom of a 13 x 9 x 2 inch greased baking pan. To the remaining flour mixture stir in cinnamon, baking soda and salt. Beat in egg, sour cream and vanilla. Stir in pineapple. Spoon mixture over crust and bake for 40 minutes, or until cake pulls away from sides of the pan. Cool completely in the pan, then dust with confectioners sugar and cut into bars.
Yields 16 to 20

RICHARD NELSON

Island Streams. Electronic Graphics by Richard Nelson.

Island streams are as much a part of the Hawaiian psyche as the ocean. Once they ran freely from every mountain top to the sea, creating waterfalls and pools along their path, irrigating taro patches. In the end they mingled with the sea, creating a cooling mixture of fresh and salt water.
In the forests the clear mountain water creates pools filled with a myriad of creatures and decaying leaves. The pools are a favorite of children of all ages who slip and slide on their mossy bottoms, and shriek at the cold.
Many streams have been diverted into ditches to feed the thirsty sugar and pineapple. But Islanders know that every care must be taken with their meandering course to the sea, because when that course is not considered and is changed, the stream has a way of reclaiming its way at the next big rain.

NANO'S PRIZEWINNING LEMON MERINGUE PIE

In 1935 Gini's grandmother entered this recipe for her favorite lemon pie in a contest and won an electric refrigerator. We think it is an outstanding recipe.

Pie Crust:
1⅓ cups flour
½ teaspoon salt
¼ cup lard
½ teaspoon vinegar
2-4 tablespoons water

Preheat oven to 450 degrees.
Combine flour and salt and cut in lard with a pastry blender until mixture resembles coarse oatmeal. Combine vinegar and water and gradually stir into flour mixture. Add only enough liquid to make dough cling together. Gather into a ball and chill dough in waxed paper. Roll out dough to fit a 9" pie pan. Prick all over with a fork. Bake for 10 to 12 minutes until nicely browned.

NANO'S PRIZEWINNING LEMON MERINGUE PIE

Filling:
1½ cups sugar
½ cup cornstarch
5 egg yolks (save the whites)
2 cups boiling water
1 tablespoon butter
1 teaspoon salt
2 lemons, juiced and grated

Meringue:
5 egg whites
½ teaspoon cream of tartar
8 tablespoons sugar

Mix all filling ingredients together except for the lemon rind. Cook over a medium heat, stirring constantly, until mixture thickens and begins to boil. Add rind and remove from the stove. Cover surface with a piece of waxed paper to prevent a skin from forming. Set aside to cool.

For meringue: Beat 5 egg whites and ½ teaspoon cream of tartar together until soft peaks form. Add 8 tablespoons of sugar one tablespoon at a time, beating well after each addition. Add ¼ of the meringue to the cooled filling and put into pie shell. Top with remaining meringue and bake in a 400 degree oven until lightly browned.
Serves 8

ALOHA MERINGUE PIE

A prize winning recipe (we agree). It is delicious.

Pie crust:
1⅓ cups unbleached flour   ½ teaspoon salt
½ cup shortening   3 to 4 tablespoons cold water

Preheat oven to 425 degrees.
Cut shortening into flour and salt with a pastry blender until dough resembles small peas. Add water gradually and mix until dough holds together. Roll out dough and line a 9" pie pan. Prick bottom and sides of dough and bake for 10 to 12 minutes, until crust is golden brown. Cool.

Filling:
1 20-ounce can crushed Hawaiian pineapple   ⅛ teaspoon salt
    packed in syrup   1 cup sour cream
¾ cup granulated sugar   3 egg yolks (save whites for meringue)
2 tablespoons flour   1 tablespoon lemon juice

ALOHA MERINGUE PIE

Drain pineapple and reserve ½ cup syrup. Combine sugar, flour and salt in medium saucepan. Stir in crushed pineapple, reserved syrup, sour cream, egg yolks and lemon juice. Stirring constantly, cook over medium heat until mixture boils and thickens. Cover and cool to lukewarm. Then pour into the baked pie shell.

Meringue:
8 tablespoons granulated sugar
1 tablespoon cornstarch
½ cup water
3 egg whites

⅛ teaspoon salt
½ teaspoon cream of tartar
½ teaspoon vanilla
¼ cup chopped macadamia nuts.

Combine 2 tablespoons sugar, cornstarch and water in a small saucepan. Cook over medium heat, stirring constantly, until mixture is thick and clear. Cool.
Beat egg whites with salt, vanilla and cream of tartar until soft peaks form. Add 6 tablespoons of sugar gradually, beating well after each addition. Add cornstarch mixture and beat until meringue stands in stiff peaks. Spread evenly over pie and sprinkle with chopped macadamia nuts.
Bake for 12 to 15 minutes at 350 degrees until golden brown.
Serves 8

CRYSTALLIZED GINGER PARFAIT

There is a lot of unusual texture in this. The heat of the ginger with ice cream is wonderful!

½ gallon vanilla ice cream
½ to ¾ cup of crystallized ginger
1 cup heavy cream, whipped
¾ cup slivered almonds, toasted

Soften ice cream at room temperature for about 20 minutes. Finely chop the ginger with a sharp knife. Machines won't work. In 6 or 8 parfait glasses, or a pretty glass bowl, layer ice cream and ginger alternately 3 times. Top with whipped cream and then almonds. Return to freezer. This can be stored for several days. Take out and let sit for 10 minutes before serving.
Serves 6 to 8

LIGHT LILIKOI CHEESECAKE

Everyone just loves this dessert. It came to us via Australia.

5 ounces macadamia nut cookies, crushed
2½ ounces butter
1 cup frozen lilikoi juice concentrate, divided
½ cup water
1 tablespoon unflavored gelatin
12 ounces cream cheese, softened
½ cup sugar

1 tablespoon lemon juice
1 cup whipping cream
1 tablespoon sugar
1 tablespoon cornstarch
½ cup water
1 tablespoon light rum (optional)

Combine cookie crumbs and butter and press onto bottom and part way up sides of an 8" springform pan. Refrigerate 30 minutes. In a small saucepan combine ½ cup of the lilikoi concentrate, water and gelatin and heat over low heat, stirring until gelatin dissolves. Allow to cool and thicken slightly. In a large mixing bowl, beat softened cream cheese and ½ cup sugar until smooth. Beat in lemon juice and lilikoi mixture. Whip cream until stiff peaks form and fold into lilikoi mixture. Pour into prepared pan and refrigerate at least 2 hours. In a small pan combine remaining lilikoi concentrate, one tablespoon sugar, cornstarch and water and bring to a boil, stirring constantly. Remove from heat and stir in rum, if desired. Cool. Carefully spoon (not pour) glaze over firm cheesecake. Chill again until firm.
Serves 8

CARAMEL MIRANDA

Chef Mark Ellman has made his restaurant Avalon a "must" for visitors from far and wide and this dessert is one of his special creations. The flavors and textures of this particular ice cream, sauce and fruits are important. Please don't substitute, at least until you have tasted it once this way.

4 ounces macadamia nut ice cream,
   homemade or Häagen Daz
Choose 4 to 6 of the following:
2 ounces fresh coconut, toasted
2 ounces Maui pineapple, cubed
2 ounces star fruit, sliced
2 ounces figs, quartered
2 ounces raspberries
2 ounces strawberries

2 ounces blueberries
2 ounces cherimoya, cubed
2 ounces apple banana, sliced
Caramel Sauce:
11 ounces sugar (1⅝ cups)
5½ ounces water (⅔ cup)
1 teaspoon cream of tartar
8 ounces heavy cream
1 teaspoon butter

Whisk together in a heavy sauce pan the sugar, water, cream of tarter and cook over high heat until coppery brown. Remove from heat and whisk in cream, whisking until cool. Whisk in butter and keep at room temperature. For each serving lace some sauce on ovenproof plate. Sprinkle fruit over caramel and heat until hot. Remove and spoon ice cream in center and serve immediately.

PINEAPPLE UPSIDE DOWN CAKE

Here on Maui we use fresh, locally grown pineapple for this ever-popular dessert.

⅓ cup butter, melted
1 cup firmly packed brown sugar
2 cups fresh pineapple, cut into ½ inch chunks
1½ cups all purpose flour
1½ teaspoons baking powder
½ teaspoon salt

½ teaspoon cinnamon
½ cup butter, softened
⅔ cup granulated sugar
2 large eggs
1 teaspoon vanilla
¾ cup milk

Preheat oven to 350 degrees.
Drain the pineapple chunks and pat until very dry using paper towels. Mix butter and sugar together and put into a 9" square by 2" deep cake pan. Arrange pineapple on top. Sift together flour, baking powder, salt and cinnamon. Set aside. In a separate bowl beat the butter with the sugar until light and fluffy. Add eggs one at a time beating well after each addition. Beat in vanilla. Beat in the flour mixture, alternating with the milk, ending with the flour mix. Pour batter into pan and bake in the middle of the oven for 45 to 55 minutes. Let rest for 15 minutes and then turn out onto a serving plate. Serve warm with whipped cream.
Yields 9 pieces

KAHALA COCONUT CAKE

A light and lovely cake, Serve it at your next luau.

Cake:
4 eggs, separated
½ cup vegetable oil
½ cup water
½ teaspoon vanilla
½ teaspoon salt
¾ cup sugar
1 cup cake flour
Pinch of cream of tartar

Filling:
1 cup milk
1½ teaspoons cornstarch
1 large egg, beaten
⅓ cup sugar
¼ teaspoon vanilla

Frosting:
1 cup heavy cream
2 tablespoons powdered sugar
1 package shredded coconut

KAHALA COCONUT CAKE

Preheat oven to 325 degrees.

Cake: grease and flour 2-8" square cake pans.

Mix egg yolks, oil, water and vanilla. Add salt, sugar and flour and mix until smooth.

Beat egg whites and cream of tartar until firm and fold carefully into batter.

Pour into cake pans and bake for 30 minutes, or until cake tests done.

Remove from pans and cool.

Filling: mix 1 tablespoon of the milk with cornstarch and mix with beaten eggs.

Bring remainder of milk, sugar and vanilla to a boil.

Add cornstarch mixture to boiling milk, stirring until thick. Cool.

Spread custard between the layers of cake.

Frosting: frost sides and top of cake with sweetened whipped cream.

And top generously with shredded coconut. Chill ½ hour before serving.

Serves 8

ORANGE MARMALADE SOUFFLÉ

Gini says "Every man I've ever served this to wanted to take me home to meet his mother. Fortunately, I already have a mother-in-law."

¼ cup Grand Marnier
1 tablespoon lemon juice
1 tablespoon unflavored gelatin
5 eggs, separated
1 cup sugar, divided
¾ cup fresh orange juice
½ cup orange marmalade
¼ teaspoon salt
½ teaspoon grated lemon peel
1½ cups whipping cream, whipped
Candied orange peel

Sauce:
1 cup milk
2 tablespoons butter
⅓ cup sugar, divided in half
2 egg yolks
1 tablespoon cornstarch
½ teaspoon vanilla
¼ cup Grand Marnier
¼ cup whipping cream, whipped

To make soufflé, combine ¼ cup Grand Marnier and lemon juice in a small bowl. Sprinkle gelatin over the top and let soften. Combine egg yolks, ¾ cup of the sugar, orange juice, marmalade and salt in the top of a double boiler. Cook over low heat until mixture thickens. Remove from heat and stir in gelatin mixture and lemon peel. Cool to room temperature.

ORANGE MARMALADE SOUFFLÉ

Beat egg whites until foamy, stir in remaining ¼ cup sugar, and continue beating until stiff peaks form. Alternately fold egg whites and whipped cream into gelatin mixture. Pour into a 2 quart soufflé dish and refrigerate until firm. Decorate with candied orange peel.

To make sauce: Combine milk, butter and half of the sugar in a pan and bring to a boil over medium heat. Set aside. With electric mixer, beat egg yolks and remaining sugar in a small bowl until lemon colored. Gradually beat in ½ cup milk mixture, then add to the remaining milk mixture, whisking until blended. Place over moderate heat and bring to a boil. Remove from heat and stir in vanilla. Refrigerate until chilled. Just before serving, slowly warm the sauce and stir in Grand Marnier and whipped cream. Serve over soufflé.

Serves 10 to 12

SUE KWON'S WONDERFUL CRANBERRY PIE

This pie is famous because everyone was talking about it after she served it at a party and because she was understandably reluctant to part with the recipe. However, we persevered. Plan ahead, you need two days to make this pie.

Pie Crust:
2½ cups all purpose flour
4 tablespoons packed brown sugar
1 tablespoon ground ginger
Pinch of salt
8 tablespoons cold unsalted butter

4 tablespoons shortening, or unsalted margarine
4-5 tablespoons cold apple juice
1 egg
1 tablespoon water
    (Mix egg and water together for the egg wash
    to brush on top of crust)

Put all ingredients except the apple juice, egg and water, into a food processor and pulse until mixture looks like coarse corn meal. Add apple juice a tablespoon at a time until mixture just forms a ball. Wrap in plastic wrap and refrigerate overnight.

SUE KWON'S WONDERFUL CRANBERRY PIE

Filling:
8 cups of fresh cranberries (2 bags)
Zest of 2 oranges, grated
½ cup Grand Marnier or any orange
　flavored liqueur
1 cup Creme de Cassis liqueur

1¾ cups sugar
⅓ cup cornstarch
½ cup minced candied ginger
1 large egg
1 tablespoon water

Mix together the cranberries, orange zest, Grand Marnier and Creme de Cassis. Cover and let sit at room temperature overnight.

The next day, drain liquid from cranberries into a medium saucepan. Add sugar and cornstarch. Heat, stirring constantly until thick and translucent. Pour over berries and stir in chopped ginger.

Preheat oven to 350 degrees.

Divide dough in half. Roll out half to line deep a 9" dish pie plate. Pour filling in. Roll out remaining crust and cut into ½" strips to make lattice topping. Crimp edges and brush on egg wash. Place on cookie sheet to catch drips and bake pie about 1 hour, or until the top is golden and the filling is bubbling. Cool to room temperature and serve.

CHOCOLATE PEANUT BUTTER PIE

The ideal dessert, a rich and elegant flavor and a snap to prepare. It can be served chilled or frozen.

For the crust:
1¾ cups chocolate wafer cookie crumbs
3 tablespoons sugar
5 tablespoons unsalted butter, melted
Filling:
8 ounces cream cheese, softened

1 cup creamy peanut butter
1 cup sugar
1½ cups well-chilled heavy cream
Topping:
½ cup heavy cream
6 ounces semisweet chocolate chips

Preheat oven to 350 degrees.
In a bowl blend together well the cookie crumbs, the sugar, and the butter. Press the mixture onto the bottom and up the side of a 9" pie plate and bake for 10 minutes. Let crust cool.
Using a large bowl beat cream cheese with peanut butter until mixture is smooth. Add sugar and combine well. In a chilled bowl beat the cream until it holds soft peaks. Fold one fourth of it into the peanut butter mixture to lighten it, and then fold in the remaining cream gently but thoroughly. Mound filling in the crust and chill, covered, for at least 4 hours or overnight.
In a small, heavy saucepan bring the cream to a boil and remove pan from heat. Add the chocolate, stirring until mixture is smooth. Let topping cool for 15 to 20 minutes, or until it is cool to the touch. Pour topping evenly over the pie and chill for 30 minutes, or until topping is set.
Serves 8

COFFEE JELLY

This is an old-fashioned dessert which has sprung up again in unexpected places - from an elegant restaurant in Los Angeles to the Kabuki Theater in Tokyo, where it is featured as a "specialty."

1 package unflavored gelatin
1¾ cups hot, strong brewed coffee
2 tablespoons Kahlua or brandy, optional

½ pint whipping cream
Hawaiian raw sugar
   or plain white granulated sugar

Soften gelatin on ¼ cup water. Pour the hot coffee onto the gelatin and stir until gelatin has dissolved. Add Kahlua or brandy, if desired. Pour into individual saucers and refrigerate until firm
To serve: Pour cold heavy cream on each to cover the gelatin and top with a sprinkle of crunchy sugar. Serve immediately. Or, as they do in Tokyo, top with sweetened whipped cream.
Serves 4

BEN KIKUYAMA

The Mango Stand. Mixed Media by Ben Kikuyama.

They sat along the roadsides. Golden ovals with bits of rose and green, the pile of mangoes beckoned drivers who would stop, select one or two to eat on the road, or peel for a fruit salad later. There was only the honor system. Coins were deposited in a tin sitting on the small table beside the mangoes. No one would have thought of cheating-of taking without giving back.
The stand on Front Street in Lahaina was a bit more substantial. Its board front was stained a deep green. It was the same green of most of the houses in town.
Children loved the mango stand, but not especially for the mangoes which they could get anytime in their own yards. They wanted the sticky, sweet candy and the sweet sour Chinese seeds in small cellophane packages which were stacked beside the healthier produce.
The stand seemed like an oasis in the hot Lahaina afternoons. It was a place to spend your loose change; a place you'd always remember.

CHRISTMAS TREATS

Not so very long ago Maui was a sleepy little island. We ordered our children's Christmas toys from the Sears catalog and prayed that they would get here in time. We had no gourmet shops to pop into to pick up a special delicacy and the mail order catalog business of today was in its infancy. So, we made things for each other, using ingredients that were readily available, which we exchanged at Christmastime. We all had our specialties, and the holidays would not seem complete without a sampling of each.

Gini made a white fruit cake laden with candied pineapple and macadamia nuts. None of our children liked the traditional dark cake soaked in rum, but this cake was heaven.

Zelie made stollen from her mother-in-law's recipe. It was, of course, before electric bread makers, and batch after batch had to be worked by hand and baked in an already hot "down country" kitchen. A real labor of love.

Carol made crisp, succulent spiced walnuts. These held up in our hot, humid climate, and didn't stick together, even though they did have some sugar in the coating.

Penny always made cookies and candies, using some of her mother's recipes. The coconut dreams are at least a two generation tradition and always a part of Penny's Christmas goodies box.

Judy Bisgard, a real child of the islands, delighted her friends with jellies, chutneys and Prune Mui.

Judy Furtado, lovingly known as the queen of rich and sinfully indulgent foods, combined egg yolks, butter and passion fruit juice into a curd to die for. We'd like to share these treasured recipes with you, along with several we added in later years.

LYMAN'S CHILI PEPPER WATER

The Hawaiian chili pepper is very important in our diet. We use it in cooking, but more pervasive is the bottle of Chili Pepper Water. It is found on many Island tables, along with a bottle of shoyu, to be sprinkled liberally on whatever is served. Each family has it's own recipe and it's own pepper bush. This recipe came from Judy's Uncle Arthur and it is "the best".

1 cup water
50 whole red Hawaiian chilies
½ tablespoon Hawaiian salt
½ tablespoon rice vinegar

Combine all ingredients in a small saucepan and boil gently, uncovered, for 30 minutes. Put into a blender and blend until the peppers are liquefied. Do not strain. Pour everything into a bottle (a rinsed out ketchup or Worcestershire sauce bottle is perfect.)
This makes extra, extra hot sauce. For medium hot use 35 chilies. For regular hot use 25 chilies. When boiling chilies be sure that your kitchen is well ventilated as the fumes are intense!

SMOKED SALMON PATÉ

Elegant holiday fare and a welcomed gift.

1¼ pounds smoked salmon
   (Atlantic, Scottish or Norwegian)
3 sticks unsalted butter (1½ cups)

1 tablespoon lemon juice
⅓ cup heavy cream
⅛ teaspoon cayenne

In a food processor blend salmon in batches with butter, lemon juice and cream until mixture is smooth. Line a pate mold (11½ x 3¼ x 2½) with plastic wrap. Spread salmon in mold and chill for at least 8 hours. Serve in thin slices with toast points or crackers.
Serves 18

CURRIED CHINESE WALNUTS

The "crunch" is wonderful, sweet and savory at the same time.

1 pound walnut halves, or large pieces
½ cup sugar
2½ tablespoons corn oil
½ teaspoon salt
¼ teaspoon pepper
¼ teaspoon cayenne pepper

1¼ teaspoons ground cumin
¼ teaspoon coriander
½ teaspoon ginger
¼ teaspoon ground cloves
½ teaspoon chili powder

Blanch walnuts in boiling water for 1 minute. Drain well.
While still hot, put in a bowl and toss with the sugar and corn oil. Let stand 10 minutes.
Arrange in a single layer on a rimmed baking sheet.
Bake 30 to 35 minutes, turning every 5 to 10 minutes. When nuts are brown and crispy, put into a bowl.
Combine seasonings and toss with still warm nuts. Spread in a single layer to cool.
Store in airtight container.
Yields 4 to 5 cups

GRANDMA HARDERS' CHRISTMAS STOLLEN

Zelie has been making this for her friends for Christmas for years. Children who have grown up with it for Christmas breakfast are now returning home for the holidays and bringing their children. We were afraid one day Zelie would say "Enough!"- so we begged her for the recipe.

2½ cups milk
1 teaspoon salt
1½ cup butter
1 cup sugar
½ cup honey
1 cup warm water
1 teaspoon honey or sugar
5 tablespoons yeast
4 eggs
4 cups flour
2½ tablespoons cinnamon
1½ tablespoons mace
1½ tablespoons nutmeg
1½ tablespoons cardamon

4 cups flour
3 cups raisins
1 cup citron or glazed orange rind,
   coarsely chopped
1 teaspoon grated orange rind
1 teaspoon grated lemon rind
1 teaspoon almond extract
1 cup chopped almonds

Frosting:
l pound powdered sugar
½ cup butter
½ teaspoon almond extract
¼ cup water or milk

GRANDMA HARDERS' CHRISTMAS STOLLEN

Scald first 5 ingredients, then cool to luke warm.

Mix together the warm water, honey and yeast and allow to rise (about 5 minutes).

In a large bowl beat 4 eggs. Add cooled milk mixture and yeast mixture. Add 4 cups flour and the spices and beat well with dough hook.

Add 4 more cups of flour, and remaining ingredients and beat well.

Transfer dough to a large oiled bowl and let rise until doubled. Punch down. Remove portions of dough to floured board, knead a bit more flour in, flatten into a rectangle, dot top with butter, brown sugar and cinnamon, fold over to form stollen. According to German tradition, folding the loaves in thirds represents the baby Christ child's bunting with the white frosting the snow on it.

Let it rise on greased pans until doubled, about 45 minutes to an hour. Bake at 325 degrees about 30 minutes or until tops are nicely browned. When cool top with frosting. Frosting: Beat together the powdered sugar, butter, almond extract and water or milk.

Yields 10 small loaves or 5 large loaves

PASSION FRUIT CURD

What a joy to have in the refrigerator during the busy holiday season. Use as a filling for a layer cake, or lighten with some whipped cream and serve on meringue shells, or you can just eat it by the spoonful right out of the jar.

1 cup sugar

6 tablespoons unsalted butter

½ cup frozen concentrated passion fruit juice

1 tablespoon grated lemon or orange zest

3 eggs

1 egg yolk

Thaw juice, measure ½ cup and cook this in the top part of a double boiler until reduced to ⅓ cup. Place pan over simmering water in the bottom of the double boiler, add sugar, butter and zest. Cook, stirring constantly, until the sugar melts. Beat eggs and the egg yolk together and strain into the hot mixture stirring constantly for 15 to 20 minutes, or until the mixture thickens. Pour into a festive glass or mug and refrigerate. Keeps well for up to 3 weeks in the refrigerator.
Yields 2 cups

PRUNE MUI

Prune Mui almost defies description unless you are familiar with Chinese "seeds". This is an adaptation that we think came about during World War II when Chinese seeds were temporarily not imported. Our friend, Honeybun, shared her recipe with Judy. Prune Mui is an addictive snack for Island kids of every age.

1 pound dark brown sugar
3 tablespoons Hawaiian rock salt
3 tablespoons bourbon
⅛ teaspoon Chinese five spice

2 cups fresh lemon juice
8 12-ounce packages pitted prunes
2 packages dried apricots
2 ounces seedless Li Hing Mui

Combine and mix well the sugar, salt, bourbon, five spice and lemon juice in a large covered container. Toss in prunes, apricots and Li Hing Mui, cover and let stand, refrigerated, for four days, mixing twice a day. Makes 1 gallon. Prepare for gift giving as you would any preserve, in sterilized bottles, sealed in a water bath.
Yields 3 quarts

COCONUT DREAMS

Follow instructions carefully and you will end up with a delicious chewy, buttery, apricot candy covered in coconut.

1 cup water
18 dried apricot halves
2 cups sugar
⅛ teaspoon salt

2 tablespoons butter
1 teaspoon vanilla
1 cup shredded coconut

Put water and apricot halves into a small saucepan. Cover and simmer over very low heat until very soft. Add sugar, salt and butter. Cook over low heat to 238 degrees on a candy thermometer, or soft ball stage if you are using the old fashioned method of drizzling a bit of the mixture into a small cup of ice water. Remove from heat. Add vanilla and cool to 110 degrees or just cool enough to touch. Drop by teaspoonful onto coconut which you have spread onto a large flat surface, a cookie sheet is good. Roll until well covered. You must work quite quickly as the mixture becomes too firm to work with if allowed to cool too much. These can be eaten immediately, refrigerated, or frozen.
Yields 3 dozen

WHITE MACADAMIA NUT FRUITCAKE

Not your traditional holiday fruitcake. This is more like an elegant pound cake.

2 7-ounce jars whole macadamia nuts
16 ounces candied pineapple,
    cut into small wedges
16 ounces maraschino cherries, drained
4 cups flour, sifted and divided
1½ cups butter, softened

2 cups granulated sugar
6 eggs, separated
¾ cup orange juice
1 teaspoon grated orange rind
2 tablespoons finely chopped candied ginger
1 teaspoon cream of tartar

Preheat oven to 275 degrees.
Generously butter two 8½ x 4½ inch loaf pans. In a large bowl combine macadamia nuts, pineapple and cherries with ½ cup of the flour. Toss gently. Cream butter and sugar until light and fluffy. Beat egg yolks and add to butter mixture and blend thoroughly. Add orange juice alternately with remaining flour. Blend well and fold in orange rind, candied ginger and macadamia nut-fruit mixture. Beat egg whites together with cream of tartar until stiff and glossy. Fold into batter and spoon batter into prepared pans. Bake 1½ to 2 hours or until cakes test done. They should have a pale golden brown color on top. Cover with foil if they seem to be browning too quickly.
Yields 2 loaves

AL LAGUNERO

Shua Me Ka Ono. Watercolor by Al Lagunero.

It's the oldest thing you can imagine, sitting before a fire. The fish you caught earlier is turning a toasty color and the smell begins to make you hungrier than you thought.

The style of cooking is called pulehu. It means to grill. Only when you add being outside watching the charcoal glow flare up and down, it's almost primeval. You sense that Hawaiians have been doing this very thing for centuries.

A firm, green breadfruit brought from the neighbor's yard is in there, too. It's tucked in near the coals ready to be broken open when it's cooked; it's starchy flesh eaten as a complement to the fish. "It's so old,"says the artist, speaking of the pulehu fish technique,"but we still do it."

RESTAURANTS

Times are changing. Our children are pretty much all grown up and out of the nest. The bounty of the land is not as available as it used to be. You can't just pick fruit you see by the side of the road any more as it might be someone's cash crop that they are counting on to sell. We all have gotten busy with careers or volunteer work and travels and find that we are less likely to cook for our friends, now that it is so easy to suggest trying out the latest new restaurant. Hawaii Regional Cooking is "in" and it is exciting to watch it develop.

So, it seemed particularly appropriate to end this book with a section sampling from some of our favorite restaurants. Some have been feeding Maui residents and visitors since before World War II. But most of the chefs have come into their own in the last fifteen years. Each has an individual style. And they all belong on your "must try" list.

KIHATA'S CHICKEN KARAAGE

Kihata's 117 Hana Highway, Paia.
Mr. Kihata came from Japan. After many steps he landed in Paia, Maui operating his own place.
This is one of his easy and quick appetizers.

1 pound boneless skinless chicken thighs
½ cup potato starch
Cooking oil
Base sauce:
½ cup water
1 tablespoon shoyu
1 tablespoon sake
½ teaspoon ginger, finely ground

Ponzu sauce:
¼ cup vinegar
¼ cup shoyu
2 tablespoons water
⅓ teaspoon dashinomoto:
    fish flavored soup stock

Preheat cooking oil to 150 to 170 degrees Celsius, 300-338 degrees Farenheit.
Cut each chicken thigh into 5 to 6 bite size pieces and let soak in base sauce for 2 minutes. Squeeze off excess sauce and generously cover chicken pieces in potato starch. Shake off excess starch and deep fry. Cook until slightly golden brown. Dip in ponzu sauce and serve over a bed of lettuce.
Serves 4

TEQUILA SHRIMP WITH FIRE CRACKER RICE

David Paul's 127 Lahainaluna Road, Lahaina.
David Paul's is an extraordinarily beautiful restaurant in the center of Lahaina town. Newly renovated, it is an upscale, fun place to people watch, partake of great wines, and experience innovative cuisine.

Tequila Shrimp:

1 pound shelled and deveined shrimp (16-20)	1 Serrano chili, finely chopped
½ cup Cuervo Gold Especial	2 tablespoons brown sugar
¼ cup fresh lime juice	Salt and pepper to taste
¼ cup salad oil	Dash of cumin
3 tablespoons fresh cilantro, chopped	2 tablespoons softened butter
4 cloves garlic, pressed	2 tablespoons chilled butter

Butterfly back side and thoroughly wash shrimp. Marinate for at least one hour in all ingredients except for ¼ cup tequila, a pinch of chili, garlic, cilantro and chilled butter. Drain shrimp and reserve marinade. In a sauté pan on high heat, cook shrimp on both sides in butter for about one minute. Remove from pan and keep warm. Add half of the marinade to sauté pan and reduce by half over high heat. Add cold butter and remainder of tequila and spices. Flambé. Incorporate by whisking together and serve over shrimp placed around a bed of rice.

TEQUILA SHRIMP WITH FIRE CRACKER RICE

Firecracker Rice:

3 cups long grain rice (jasmine is best)

3 cups chicken or clam stock

1 vanilla pod, cut in half crosswise

1 tablespoon garlic, chopped

1 teaspoon chopped shallots,

1 tablespoon Annato seeds,
  boiled and puréed with oil

2 tablespoons Mulatto chili, chopped

2 tablespoons dried red Anaheim chili,
  toasted and julienned

1 small red chili pepper (optional)

1 cup white wine

8 tablespoons softened butter

Salt and pepper to taste

Wash rice thoroughly, place half the amount in heavy-bottom sauce pan and sauté with 2 tablespoons butter, shallots and vanilla pod. Add half the stock, half the wine and bring to a boil. Reduce heat to simmer and cover until all liquid is absorbed. Remove from heat and fluff. Sauté the remaining ingredients, except for the rice, for a minute and then cook the remaining rice in the same method. Serve a 3 ounce portion of each rice as a bed for the shrimp.

Serves 2 to 4

BLACKENED ISLAND AHI

Roy's Kahana Bar and Grill 4405 Honoapiilani Highway, Kahana.
Roy Yamaguchi is probably the most energetic innovative chef in Hawaii today and his Pacific Rim recipes will be a part of Hawaii's cuisine for the 90's and beyond.

2 pounds of fresh Ahi (7 ounces per serving)
2 ounces of Cajun spice (any brand)

Mustard Soy:
4 ounces Coleman Mustard
2 ounces hot water
2 ounces Japanese rice wine vinegar
4 ounces of soy sauce

Buerre Blanc Sauce:
2 cups white wine
¾ ounce white wine vinegar
1 tablespoon chopped Shallots
1 cup heavy cream
½ pound unsalted butter

Vegetables:
Won bok, thinly sliced
Carrots, julienne
Onions, finely cut
Choi sum or spinach
Garlic, minced
Ginger, minced

Garnish:
Black roasted seasame seeds
Kaiware sprouts
Pickled ginger

BLACKENED ISLAND AHI

Soy Mustard Sauce: Mix mustard and water together to form a paste. Add vinegar and soy sauce, strain through a fine strainer and refrigerate.

Buerre Blanc Sauce: Combine white wine, vinegar and shallots, boil over medium high flame and reduce to one cup. Add 1 cup heavy cream and reduce to ½ a cup. Then over a low flame, incorporate small cubes of the chilled unsalted butter and stir slowly (do not whip) until all of the butter has been incorporated. Salt and pepper to taste. Strain through fine mesh strainer. Yields 1½ cups.

Fish: Put the Cajun spice on a platter and dredge only half of one side of the ahi. In a heavy skillet on a very high flame sear the ahi to desired doneness, preferably medium-rare. Place fish on a bed of stir fried fresh vegetables of your choice. Sauce half of the plate with white butter sauce and the other half with the soy mustard sauce. Garnish with black roasted sesame seeds, Kaiware sprouts and pickled ginger.
Serves 4

CANARD LA PEROUSE

Chez Paul Olowalu Village Road at Honoapiilani Highway.
Situated in an unlikely spot on the edge of a cane field next to a small local market, mid-way between Maalaea and Lahaina, you will find Chez Paul. It is the first French restaurant we can remember on Maui; it is small, intimate and romantic. The food is exquisite and the service is impeccable.

4-5 pound Long Island duckling
1 cup coarsely ground bread crumbs
½ cup finely grated Gruyere cheese
Cream
Dijon mustard

Sauce:
3 tablespoons chopped shallots
2 cups Muscatel
1 quart duck velouté
½ cup cream
Salt and pepper

CANARD LA PEROUSE

Preheat oven to 475 degrees.

Unwrap a well thawed duckling and remove neck and giblets. Cut off top 2 sections of wings and knob from legs. Remove any excess fat from body cavity. Place on rack in a roasting pan and roast for 45 minutes. Pour off accumulated fat, reduce heat to 325 degrees and roast for another 45 minutes. Remove from oven and cool.

Separate duck into quarters and remove bones. Combine bread crumbs and Gruyere and moisten with cream. Paint duck skin liberally with Dijon mustard. Press on bread crumbs and cheese.

Preheat oven to 450 degrees.

Place two loose balls of tin foil on a sizzle platter. Lay duck pieces on top of foil, crumb side up. Place in oven and roast for 7 to 12 minutes until golden brown.

For Sauce: Reduce shallots in Muscatel until 3 tablespoons of liquid remain. Add velouté, bring to boil over medium heat. Add cream, salt and pepper.

BROILED GARLIC PRAWNS ON TOMATO VINAIGRETTE

Maui Prince Hotel-Prince Court 5400 Makena Alanui, Makena.
On one of Maui's best beaches, the Maui Prince Hotel is the only hotel in the peaceful, unspoiled Makena area. Executive Chef Roger Dikon has experimented with local fruits and vegetables and created many wonderful dishes. He has been widely recognized for his great contributions to the Pacific Rim cuisine.

2 pounds fresh Kahuku Prawns,
  peeled and deveined
¼ cup minced fresh garlic
½ cup macadamia nut oil
4 tablespoon minced fresh chives

Chunky Tomato Vinaigrette:
2 large ripe tomatoes, diced
¼ cup Maui onions, minced

2 tablespoons fresh herbs of choice:
  thyme, cilantro, parsley
½ teaspoon garlic, minced
⅓ teaspoon Hawaiian salt
3 tablespoons Balsamic vinegar
Fresh ground pepper
⅓ cup fresh chopped basil
2 tablespoons virgin olive oil

BROILED GARLIC PRAWNS ON TOMATO VINAIGRETTE

Avocado Butter:
1 whole ripe avocado
Salt to taste
3 tablespoons fresh lime juice
4 tablespoons of virgin olive oil

Marinate the prawns in the garlic, macadamia oil and chives mixture for 30 minutes.
Mix all ingredients for the vinaigrette together and set aside.
Blend avocado in a food processor, adding salt, lime juice and olive oil to taste. Set aside.
Broil prawns under high heat and serve on bed of fresh tomato vinaigrette with avocado butter.

PEPPER BROILED AHI WITH PAPAYA SALSA

Mama's Fish House 799 Poho Place, Kuau.
Off Hana Highway, just past Paia, you'll find this breezy, open restaurant right on the beach, serving the freshest of fish prepared in a variety of wonderful ways. It is a perfect spot to while away a hot midday - under the shade of the coconut palms, watching the colorful windsurfers just off shore.

Papaya Salsa:
1 large, firm, ripe papaya
1 large red bell pepper
1 tablespoon fresh chopped mint leaves
1 tablespoon fresh chopped cilantro
2 tablespoons fresh lime juice

4 fresh Ahi filets
2 tablespoons olive oil

Green Peppercorn Sauce:
¼ cup olive oil
½ cup green peppercorns in brine
   (do not add the brine)
1 tablespoon black peppercorns
¼ cup fresh basil
2 cloves garlic

PEPPER BROILED AHI WITH PAPAYA SALSA

First prepare the salsa.

Peel and seed one large, firm, ripe papaya. Cut in ½ inch cubes. Roast one large red bell pepper on grill or over direct flame until skin blackens. Peel, seed, and cut in ¼ inch dice. Gently toss together with mint leaves, cilantro and lime juice. Set aside while you prepare the fish.

Next, prepare the green peppercorn sauce.

In a food processor place ¼ cup olive oil, peppercorns, basil and garlic, blend well.

Finally, brush fish with olive oil, using as much as necessary. Grill fish lightly on one side. Turn fish and brush with the green peppercorn sauce on the other side. Continue cooking to desired doneness.

"At *Mama's* we prefer our Ahi pink inside."

Serve with plenty of fresh papaya salsa.

Serves 4

MAKAWAO STEAK HOUSE GREEK CHICKEN

Makawao Steak House 3612 Baldwin Avenue, Makawao.
In the heart of this historic paniolo town, the Furtados have taken the old Iwaishi Store, and made it into a cozy upcountry haven. It is worth a special trip to Makawao to enjoy their creative island dishes.

8 8-ounce boneless chicken breasts
Spinach mixture:
3 10-ounce boxes frozen spinach (thawed)
1 tablespoon olive oil
1½ tablespoons minced garlic
1½ tablespoons minced shallots
1 tablespoon leaf oregano

½ cup lemon juice
2 tablespoons feta cheese
2 tablespoons chopped black olives
Lemon sauce:
1 cup melted butter
2 tablespoons lemon juice
2 tablespoons heavy cream

Sauté ingredients in spinach mixture 8 to 10 minutes. Salt and pepper to taste. Remove from heat and strain to remove most of the liquid. Remove most of the skin from the breasts leaving a 2 inch strip down the center. Lay out breast skin side down and layer with spinach mixture, feta and olives. Roll up with seam on the underneath side. Lightly flour and brown breasts in skillet until skin is crispy. Remove to baking sheet and bake for 20 minutes at 350 degrees. Whisk lemon sauce in small sauce pan just until hot (don't allow to separate). Spoon 2 tablespoons of lemon sauce onto each individual plate, place chicken breast on top and serve immediately.
Serves 8

FROZEN HAWAIIAN CHOCOLATE SOUFFLÉ

Gerard's Restaurant 174 Lahainaluna Road, Lahaina.
Tucked away on a side street in Lahaina, on the lower floor of the Plantation Inn, is Gerard's - with elegant food, a sophisticated atmosphere, Country French decor and cool tropical evening breezes. Maui residents from all parts of the Island soon discovered the allure of this restaurant and have been loyal patrons for years and years.

5 ounces Hawaiian chocolate
8 ounces heavy cream
2 whole eggs

The night before, boil the cream for one minute in a small thick sauce pan, stirring with a whip. Keep aside. Add the chocolate pistoles mixing well until smooth consistency. Cover and refrigerate for 12 hours. The next day, separate the egg whites from the yolks. Add the egg yolks to the chocolate preparation, whip the egg whites firm and mix delicately into the above preparation. Line the outside of a soufflé bowl with a 5 inch high wax paper collar tied with a string around the bowl. Pour the chocolate mixture in it and freeze for 2 hours. Remove string and paper delicately before serving.
Serves 4

OPAKAPAKA IN CAMICIA

Casanova Italian Restaurant and Deli 1188 Makawao Avenue, Makawao.
A fun crowd gathers here at the cross-roads of Makawao town to enjoy real Italian food cooked by
real Italians.

2 pounds Opakapaka
6 large leaves of romaine lettuce
4 leaves of fresh sage
1 bunch of fresh rosemary
1 bunch of Italian parsley
2 cloves garlic
Black pepper, coarsely ground
½ lemon
2 cups white wine

Garnish:
Lemon slices
Red and yellow bell peppers

Sauce:
4 tablespoons olive oil
2 garlic cloves
Salt at pleasure
2 lemons
1 bunch of Italian parsley
1 cup white wine
1 cup clam juice or fish bouillon
1 teaspoon butter

OPAKAPAKA IN CAMICIA

Preheat oven to 400 degrees.
Quickly blanch the romaine leaves in boiling water and set on a baking tray brushed with olive oil.
Clean the fish fillets and lay on romaine leaves.
Finely chop all fresh herbs, garlic and spices and sprinkle on top of fish.
Slice thinly the lemon and lay slices on the fish. Wrap the leaves tightly.
Insert in preheated oven and bake for 10 minutes.
Pour the white wine over the fish and bake for 8 more minutes.
Remove and set on serving tray.
Sauce: In a saucepan, sauté olive oil and garlic cloves till blond.
Remove garlic and add the juice of two lemons, the white wine, the clam juice and the chopped parsley.
Let it simmer till reduced by half, then add the butter rolled in a handful of white flour.
Let it melt till you reach the desired thickness of the sauce.
Pour the sauce on the fish, once laid in platter.
Decorate with slices of lemon, alternate with red and yellow julienne peppers.
Slice the loaf in 4 parts and serve.
Serves 4

SEARED SASHIMI

Avalon Restaurant and Bar 844 Front Street, Lahaina.
In an open Lahaina courtyard setting, owner-chef Mark Ellman combines Asian and Continental flavors to create many memorable delicacies, excelling in their beautiful presentation. This fine restaurant attracts many celebrities.

8 ounce piece of yellow fin Ahi
   (sashimi grade, eye only)
1 tablespoon macadamia nut oil

Herbs chopped and mixed:
2 tablespoons basil
2 tablespoons mint
2 tablespoons cilantro

Sauce:
4 ounces Chenin Blanc
2 ounces shiitake mushrooms, sliced
½ ounce ginger root, chopped
¼ ounce garlic, chopped
¼ ounce Kula onion, chopped
4 tablespoons butter
1 tablespoon soy sauce
1 tablespoon green onion, minced

Coat Ahi in macadamia nut oil and roll in herbs. Sear for 5 seconds on each side in a very hot pan. Remove and slice ⅛ inch bias. Reduce sauce ingredients over high heat until ½ volume. Add green onion. Nap plate and fan Ahi over sauce.
Serves 4

PRAWNS AMARETTO

Longhi's 888 Front Street, Lahaina

"Longhi's has become the 'in place' among Lahaina's cognoscenti, where gourmets and celebrities from all over the world gather together for a unique dining experience". It is the only place we know where the waiters recite the entire menu from memory, as it changes from day to day.

Four large prawns per person
Flour
½ shot brandy
½ shot of Amaretto
Splash of white wine

Fresh orange juice
Zest of orange, just a little
1 tablespoon of heavy cream
Parsley

Dip prawns lightly in flour. In a pan bring the butter "à point" then sauté the prawns, shell side down first. Remove from the pan and raise the heat. Add brandy, Amaretto, white wine, orange juice and zest. Mix well. Remove the pan from the heat and add heavy cream (have cream at room temperature) mix well and return pan to the heat for just a few minutes. Add parsley and serve.

MING YUEN SPECIAL FRIED NOODLES

Ming Yuen 162 Alamaha Street, Kahului.
Alan Ong, one of the owners of Ming Yuen and a master noodle maker-chef says: "To the Chinese, noodles are a very important part of our diet. It is a must on birthdays and other special occasions because it has come to symbolize long life. At Ming Yuen we are most known for this particular style of preparation."

6 ounce Chinese egg noodles
4 ounces won bok, cut into 2" squares
2 ounces broccoli
4 pieces straw mushrooms
3 to 4 thin slices of carrots, for color
2 ounces bamboo shoots, sliced
2 ounces chicken breast, diced
2 ounces pork, sliced
2 ounces shrimp, peeled and deveined
1 ounce char siu, sliced

1½ cups fresh chicken stock
2 teaspoons sesame oil
2 teaspoons dry sherry
¼ teaspoon white pepper
½ teaspoon salt
¼ teaspoon sugar
2 tablespoons oyster sauce
2 tablespoons light soy sauce
Cornstarch and water

MING YUEN SPECIAL FRIED NOODLES

Pour a couple of cups full of light cooking oil into wok and heat until hot. Carefully place raw meats into oil and blanch very quickly for a few seconds. Do not over cook your meats. Drain meats and oil out of wok, leaving only a teaspoon or so of oil in the wok. Replace meats into the wok.

Immediately add all your vegetables and 1½ cups of chicken stock. Add sesame oil, dry sherry, white pepper, salt and sugar. Allow the liquids to come to a boil and skim off the scum if any. Add oyster sauce and light soy sauce. Taste and correct to your liking.

Thicken sauce with a teaspoon or so of cornstarch. The sauce consistency should not be overly thick. So allow the cornstarch to thicken which takes a few seconds and if still not thick enough, then add another teaspoon or so.

Pour sauce over wok browned crispy egg noodles and serve immediately. Just about any kind of egg noodles can be used. If dry, blanch and place in wok with a little oil and lightly brown them.

Serves 1 to 2

MAUI PRINCE SALAD

An irresistible combination of island flavors created for The Makena Resort by Executive Chef Roger Dikon. Package the dressing, the walnuts and the cranberries along with serving instructions for a very welcome Christmas gift.

Dressing:
3 egg yolks
⅓ cup chopped fresh ginger
2 tablespoons shoyu
2 tablespoons rice wine vinegar
1 teaspoon sesame oil
¾ cup honey
1 teaspoon salt
2 Hawaiian chili peppers, seeded

1 tablespoon Dijon mustard
1½ cups vegetable oil
2 tablespoons water
Juice of one lemon
Caramelized Walnuts:
¾ cup walnuts
2 tablespoons Hawaiian raw sugar
2 tablespoons water
Dried cranberries

In an electric blender, blcnd egg yolks, ginger and shoyu together for 10 seconds. Add next six ingredients. Blend at low speed and slowly add the vegetable oil. As the mixture thickens, add the water, then lemon juice. Can be refrigerated for up to two weeks. To caramelized walnuts, heat water and sugar until sugar melts and turns color. Stir in walnuts and cook, stirring constantly until water evaporates. Cool on a plate. Serve the dressing on a salad of mixed greens. Top with walnuts and dried cranberries. Yields 3 cups

CHICKEN KATSU

Tokyo Tei 1063 Lower Main Street, Wailuku.
Tokyo Tei has been a local favorite for fifty years. The name was changed during World War II to Rainbow Grill and later changed back to the original Tokyo Tei. Betsy Cardoza has given us one of her favorite recipes.

8 6-8 ounce chicken breasts, boned and skinned
Salt and flour
1 egg
1 cup of milk
Panko flakes
¼ cup vegetable oil

Tonkatsu dipping sauce:
½ cup ketchup
3 tablespoons Worcestershire sauce
2 dashes Tabasco sauce

Make slits in chicken breasts with small paring knife. Salt lightly, flour lightly, dip in egg beaten with milk and dredge in Panko flakes. Sauté in oil in skillet until just done, taking care not to over cook. Serve immediately with Tonkatsu dipping sauce.
Serves 8

PANIOLO RIBS WITH HALIIMAILE BBQ SAUCE

Haliimaile General Store 900 Haliimaile Road, Haliimaile.
In the middle of a pineapple plantation, converted from a village store with its high ceilings and wood floors, you will find some of the most innovative and delicious cuisine.

6 Racks baby back ribs (about 6 pounds)
Sauce:
1 tablespoon margarine
2 medium onions, diced
3 cups ketchup
1½ cups chili sauce
½ cup cider vinegar
½ cup brown sugar

⅓ cup molasses
2 teaspoons cayenne pepper
⅓ cup Worcestershire sauce
2 teaspoons liquid smoke
½ lemon
½ lime
½ orange
Salt and pepper

Preheat oven to 400 degrees.
Place meat in roasting pan with ribs in an upright position. Cover with water. Cover pan with foil and bake for one hour. Ribs will be cooked through at this point. Remove from pan and dip in BBQ sauce. Place on prepared grill. Cook until well marked.

PANIOLO RIBS WITH HALIIMAILE BBQ SAUCE

While the meat is cooking, prepare the sauce. Melt the margarine in a 3 quart sauce pan with a heavy bottom. Add onions and cook until transparent. Add the rest of the ingredients and bring to a boil. Simmer for one hour on low heat. Serve with lots of sauce, mashed potatoes and pineapple chutney.

Fresh Pineapple chutney:
2 tablespoons margarine
1½ cups onion, chopped
3 cups diced fresh pineapple
¾ cup dark brown sugar

½ cup rice wine vinegar
3 tablespoons fresh basil, chopped
1 tablespoon Thai chili sauce
¾ cup raisins
⅛ cup grated fresh ginger

Sauté onions in margarine until translucent. Add the rest of the ingredients and cook until thick and still chunky, approximately 30 minutes. Store in airtight container.

INDEX

INDEX

INDEX

INDEX

INDEX

INDEX

INDEX